TERRORISM

TERRORISM
INTERDISCIPLINARY PERSPECTIVES

edited by

BURR EICHELMAN, M.D., Ph.D.
DAVID SOSKIS, M.D.
WILLIAM REID, M.D., M.P.H.

american psychiatric association
washington, dc

Terrorism, interdisciplinary perspectives.

Papers presented at a symposium held at Cross
Keys, Md. in Sept. 1979.
Includes bibliographical references.
Contents: The ethics of terror / Abraham Kaplan—
The psychiatrist and the terrorist / John Gunn—
Ethics in hostage encounters / Burr Eichelman
and John Lion—[etc.]
1. Terrorism—Psychological aspects—Congresses.
2. Terrorism—Congresses. 3. Hostage negotiations—
Congresses. 4. Hostages—Rehabilitation—Congresses.
5. Psychiatric ethics—Congresses. 6. Psychiatric
consultation—Congresses. I. Eichelman, Burr,
1943– . II. Soskis, David A. III. Reid, William
H., 1945– . IV. American Psychiatric Association.
[DNLM: 1. Ethics, Medical—Congresses. 2. Forensic
psychiatry—Congresses. 3. Prisoners—Psychology—
Congresses. 4. Psychiatry—Congresses. 5. Violence—
Congresses. WM 62 T328]
RC569.5.T47T47   1982   303.6′25′019   82-24393
ISBN 0-89042-109-9

Library of Congress cataloging in publication data
Main entry under title:

Printed in the U.S.A.

Contributors

EDITORS:

Burr Eichelman, M.D., Ph.D.
Associate Professor of Psychiatry
University of Wisconsin at Madison

David Soskis, M.D.
Clinical Associate Professor of Psychiatry
Temple University
Philadelphia, Pennsylvania

William Reid, M.D., M.P.H.
Associate Professor of Psychiatry
Nebraska Psychiatric Institute
University of Nebraska College of Medicine
Omaha, Nebraska

OTHER CONTRIBUTORS:

Frank Bolz, Jr.
Captain and Chief Negotiator
Hostage Negotiation Team
New York City Police Department

John Gunn, M.D.
Professor of Forensic Psychiatry
University of London
The Maudsley Hospital
Institute of Psychiatry

Conrad Hassel, M.S., J.D.
Unit Chief
Special Operations and Research Unit
F.B.I. Academy
Quantico, Virginia

Brian Jenkins, Ph.D.
Program Director
Security/Subnational Conflicts
The Rand Corporation
Santa Monica, California

Professor Abraham Kaplan, Ph.D.
Department of Philosophy
University of Haifa, Israel

John Lion, M.D.
Professor of Psychiatry
University of Maryland
Baltimore, Maryland

Frank Ochberg, M.D.
Mental Health Center
St. Lawrence Hospital
Lansing, Michigan

Martin Symonds, M.D.
Adjunct Professor
John Jay School of Law
Director of Psychological Services
New York City Police Department

Contents

Preface

At times, the process of assembling the Task Force, sponsoring the symposium, and promoting dialogue among the participants seemed to demand the delicacy of hostage negotiating. This process has been expedited greatly by the goodwill of various agencies and individuals. We particularly wish to thank the Law Enforcement Assistance Administration for its support of the Baltimore symposium and the American Psychiatric Association for its continued support of the Task Force.

Since many public agencies were involved in preparing this volume, it is important to acknowledge that the material presented by the authors reflects their own opinions and perceptions, and does not necessarily reflect agency policy or approval. The Task Force would like to thank the Federal Bureau of Investigation, the New York City Police Department, the Rand Corporation, Scotland Yard, and the Veterans Administration for allowing these individuals to participate in the Baltimore symposium and to contribute to this monograph.

We also wish to thank Lenore Terr, M.D. Her paper, "Psychic trauma in children: observations following the Chowchilla school-bus kidnapping," grew out of the presentation she made at the Baltimore symposium. The paper, which describes her experience dealing with children held hostage during a school-bus kidnapping in California, appeared in the January 1981 *American Journal of Psychiatry (Am J Psychiatry* 138:14–19, 1981).

Others in addition to the three editors gave their time and effort to the editing and preparation of this book. Anne Hartwig assisted with additional editing. Barbara Hughes provided editorial assistance in the early phases of the sections "Ethical Issues" and "The Victim." Edna Brooks-Pittman typed the manuscript.

Since the meeting on which this book is based was held under the auspices of the American Psychiatric Association, no royalties will accrue to the contributors or editors. All publication profits will be returned to the Association.

Introduction

In 1978, the American Psychiatric Association was besieged with questions, many from its own members, concerning terrorism and hostage situations. What roles should psychiatrists play in events during and after the hostage-taking? Should they be directly involved in negotiating for hostages? Further, should the Association serve as a clearinghouse for law enforcement agencies seeking psychiatrists to consult during such hostage situations? In September of that same year, the APA Council on National Affairs formed a task force to explore these and allied issues. This book is based on the work of that task force.

Elissa Benedek, M.D., was appointed chair of the new Task Force on the Psychiatric Aspects of Terrorism. Other members of the Task Force included Drs. Burr Eichelman, John Lion, Frank Ochberg, William Reid, David Soskis, and Martin Symonds. Nathaniel Apter, M.D., was appointed liaison with the APA's Committee on Ethics. Since the formation of the Task Force, the chair was shifted to Dr. Soskis, and Robert Simon, M.D., has been added to its membership.

The primary purpose of the Task Force has been to investigate aspects of terrorism directly affecting mental health professionals and then pass the information on to others. This book is part of that commitment. But thus far the principal effort in this educational process has been a multidisciplinary symposium on psychiatric aspects of terrorism, held at Baltimore, Maryland in September 1979. The symposium, funded jointly by the Law Enforcement Assistance Administration and APA, focused on four major areas, reflected in the four parts of the book: "Ethical Issues," "The Victim," "Training Law Enforcement Personnel," and "Research in Terrorism."

The symposium provided a unique opportunity for professionals from psychiatry, law enforcement, and the military to get to know each other. This kind of contact is one of the most useful means for overcoming interdisciplinary tension and prejudice, which have hindered collaborative work in the past. After each group of papers was presented, the participants joined in lively discussion. The original presentations have been edited and updated, incorporating many of these discussion comments as well as the more recent developments in each area.

In addition, the Task Force has welcomed to its meetings other professionals to share their experience in handling terrorist and hostage situations. These guests have included psychiatric consultants to the U.S. government, an Israeli psychologist who has worked with child survivors of a terrorist attack in Israel, and a psychiatrist familiar with the plight of the guards held hostage during the New Mexico prison riots of 1980. The breadth of these contacts has given the Task Force considerable insight into the area of psychiatric consultation. And Task Force members were privileged to visit the FBI Academy, to observe the training of FBI hostage negotiators.

The Task Force's initial charge was to examine the ethical implications of psychiatrist involvement in hostage situations as well as the appropriateness of the APA's participation in referring law enforcement agencies to specific psychiatrists. On these issues Task Force members represented a range of opinion. Some felt that psychiatrists should confine their activity exclusively to the patient-physician relationship. Others felt that the APA should encourage involvement of well-trained psychiatrists with law enforcement agencies. These psychiatrists, they believed, could teach law officers about psychopathology and even participate in hostage situations.

As the work of the Task Force continued and as its members met with the general membership at the national APA meetings of 1979 through 1982, the primary focus shifted to the victims of terrorism. Accordingly, the group's name was changed to the Task Force on the Psychiatric Aspects of Terrorism and Its Victims.

The Task Force members believe psychiatry's greatest expertise and experience in the field of terrorism does rest with the victim. Psychiatry has always played a role in providing clinical care to victims of such diverse trauma as natural disaster, war, rape, and spouse abuse. True, some behavioral scientists have tried to "profile" international terrorists—mainly in an attempt to predict their behavior. The Task Force, though, has chosen to concentrate its attention away from the work of these relatively few behavioral scientists to those issues that affect a broader segment of the APA membership.

Political terrorism such as the Iranian hostage situation can generate a population of victims—the hostages, their families, their friends—some of whom may need the support of mental health professionals. Moreover, during the course of a year a large community may experience several *non*political hostage events. Of course, the victims of these events need support programs too. And law enforcement officers need training in the area of psychopathology, since more than one-third of the hostage-takers in this country exhibit significant psychopathology. Thus, the Task Force has focused on (1) the mental health professional's response to hostage victims and (2) the training of and consultation to law enforcement professionals in this country. The first section of this book examines the ethics of such involvement with the law enforcement sector.

Part One

Ethical Issues

Ethical Issues

Introduction

BURR EICHELMAN, M.D., PH.D.

This section provides several different perspectives on the ethical issues terrorist and hostage situations present. Professor Kaplan's chapter examines the ethics of international terrorism as an ideology. Professor Kaplan's own philosophy, as illustrated by his chapter, is closely linked with the social and political realities of his homeland, Israel. "The Ethics of Terror" may suggest to some that hostage and terrorist situations generate a set of moral rules analogous to those of wartime.

Dr. Gunn's chapter presents his reflections on the ethical issues involved in consultation. Dr. Gunn draws on his experience as consultant to Scotland Yard. He observes that the physician's professional mantle may be very difficult to remove when consulting with a law enforcement agency. Further, in consulting to an agency one risks identification with the modes of operation of that agency, which might include the use of violence and deceit.

The chapter by Drs. Eichelman and Lion represents

the Task Force at work. "Ethics in Hostage Encounters" shows that ethics are usually shaped in discussions among professional peers. It also illustrates how this professional dialogue can be enhanced by referring to both broader-based ethics and specific situations.

This section is not definitive. But the different yet complementary perspectives do provide a sound framework for examining the difficult ethical issues posed for mental health professionals in hostage situations. As such, it is a starting point for discussing professional involvement in these situations.

1

The Ethics of Terror

ABRAHAM KAPLAN, PH.D.

The chief scandal of our age," says a recent writer on violence, "is the assassination of innocence in the name of justice."[1] This is scandal enough; what is more shameful is that we no longer acknowledge the difference between innocence and guilt. Moral degradation has corrupted not only the truth of moral judgments but also the meaning of morality.

Killing was once a sin, then it became a crime, and at last an illness. Now it is no more than a political statement. Norms of every kind have been replaced by standards of political correctness; normative assessment has given way to calculations of political effectiveness.

In the 19th century this reduction was foreshadowed by the Marxist critique of ideology. According to this critique, social norms express the interests of a class; there is no standpoint above the class struggle from which norms can be validated objectively.

In the 20th century a comparable reduction was promulgated by emotivism, which postulates that moral judgments only express the feelings and attitudes of the judge. Validity is subjective. *Who* is to judge replaces the question *how* to judge; identifications come first. Today, identities are chiefly political; ethical principles are correspondingly politicized. Morality is determined by party congresses, as it was once proclaimed by church councils.

Opposing the Communist reduction of morality is the democratic doctrine that, rather than politicizing morality, moralizes politics. Ethically, democracy is reinforced by socialist humanism, which retains a sense of the moral basis for all political aspiration.

The major naturalistic alternative to emotivism is pragmatism, which holds that a judgment of value differs from a statement of fact only in function. Values are expressed in decisions; facts constitute grounds for the decisions. In other contexts the values are grounds for other decisions. The regress is neither endless nor vicious.

Much can be said for the view that "all political problems are in the end ethical problems."[2] Ethics may underline all normative systems dealing with behavior—including not only politics but religion, law, and psychiatry, with its presuppositions about health and normality.

Political norms must rest on an ethical basis or else they express nothing but naked self-interest, and that only as blind dogma defines it. A decade ago Vietnam and Watergate heightened awareness that politics is subject to ethics, not the other way around. When political interests shifted and new loyalties and identifications emerged, the lesson so painfully learned was unlearned—indeed, it is being systematically negated. As no less a moralist than Martin Luther once observed, it all depends on whose ox is being gored.

If history records any moral progress, it is in the progressive freeing of moral judgment from the distortions of groundless subjectivism. Just over a hundred years ago, slavery was still thought morally justifiable. In retrospect, it is easy to see how economic interest clouded judgment. Today oil and ideology work to sustain acquiescence in terrorist murder. Nations have not agreed on a single measure outlawing terrorism. Yet they uniformly condemn the victims of terror for their measures in self-defense. Runaway slaves were outlawed long before slave owners were.

The fact is that in addressing the ethics of terrorism we cannot stipulate the immorality of terror. Widespread justifications for terror are being offered by terrorists and by their political supporters, who are contemptuous of what they call "colonialist" or "establishment" morality.

The terrorist ethic (or lack of it) is revealed in the semantics of "claiming" responsibility for an act of terror rather than "confessing" it. The claim enhances the image of the terrorist group's effectiveness, especially as compared with rival groups. It also serves to make the group more terrifying in the eyes of the target. No cowardice or cruelty shames the act of terror; on the contrary, terrorists take pride in their performance.

Political semantics are notoriously irresponsible. Labeling an act "terror" does not make it so, but merely may make people think it so. The term *terror* should not be applied to all violence of which the speaker disapproves. In such usage the moral condemnation of the act is assured, but the judgment is tautologous. Supporters of terrorist acts may so restrict the label that in their usage there is no such thing as an act of terror at all. Moral discrimination calls for more discriminating semantics.

Violence constitutes an act of terror when its victims are distinct from its target—those being coerced. The distance between target and victim varies from direct agents of the target (in political terror, diplomats, police, soldiers, officials) to totally uninvolved bystanders.

The distinction between target and victim may correspondingly differentiate the aim of the violence—what the terrorist wants the target to do, the reason for the act of terror—from the demands of the violence, which determine how the terrorist will dispose of his victims. Demands might not be made at all, as in the case of a bomb left in a crowded marketplace, or as in the case of indiscriminate shooting (such as the "Zebra" killings in California). When demands are made, the terrorist may even want them refused—the better to attain his aims—and may therefore escalate his demands until they are quite unacceptable.

That terrorism claims innocent victims follows from its definition. Passengers on commercial airliners, customers of banks, department stores, and supermarkets, pedestrians and school children cannot be regarded as agents of political targets except in a sense so broad that agency loses its meaning.

The morality of terrorism is not prejudged by the definition. Terrorists and their supporters repudiate the principle of democratic legal philosophy that "better ten guilty persons escape than one innocent suffer,"[3] replacing it by its converse, that victimizing the innocent is justified if, through the victimization, the guilty are made to suffer. They may hold instead that the victims are not truly innocent, thereby blurring the distinction between victim and target, and so denying that the act was terroristic at all.

All violence evokes fear that coerces the target. The bank robber uses his gun to terrify the teller; a military action may destroy not the enemy's military capacity, but his will to resist. But unless the victims of an act are distinguished from its targets, the act cannot be called terroristic.

The distinction is not always easily drawn. Bystanders may become *unintended victims* (a passerby hit by a ricocheting bullet) or *incidental victims* (a bystander used as a shield by a criminal caught in a police shoot-out). The difference lies in the intent. Terrorists intentionally involve victims, so as to produce the fear meant to coerce the target. That their deeds may also produce unintended and incidental victims is often part of their plan, so as to intensify the fearfulness of the target.

Moral confusion is engendered by situations in which there are unintended victims, whose presence is thought to make the act terroristic. Seizing hostages is one thing; unintentionally killing bystanders in actions combatting terror is quite another. Refugee camps serving also as terrorist bases may be targets of nonterrorist action. When armed groups station their military installations in civilian settings they risk innocent deaths. Thereby civilians are being held hostage. Attacks on such installations cannot be called terrorist simply because there are civilian casualties. These victims are altogether unintended.

Not every act of violence by a terrorist is a terrorist act. What is produced may be only linked violence: violence as linked violence is violence as a condition or consequence of the act of terror—such as robbing a bank to finance terrorist operations or killing bystanders in making a getaway from an act of terror. The morality of linked violence depends on the acts to which it is linked, as well

as on the nature of the linkage. In American legal practice, deaths brought about in committing a felony, however unintended or incidental they may be, are accounted
murder.

The question is not where to draw the line between
terror and other forms of violence; there is no line to be
drawn. Intermediate cases abound in which victims are
not direct agents of the target yet are not wholly disso-
ciated from the target either. These are symbolic victims,
like a former political figure (Alberto Moro), or like the
leader of the Teheran Jewish community executed on
charges of Zionism. The Israeli athletes murdered at the
Olympic Games are also symbolic victims.

The justification is sometimes offered that terror is the
sole recourse of those who face a hopelessly superior power
subjecting them to despotism or enslavement. Most terror, however, has been used by the powerful against the
powerless—witness the reigns of terror of Robespierre and
Danton, of Hitler, Mussolini, and Stalin; of Moamar Qua-
dafi, Idi Amin, and the Ayatollah Khomeini.

Those protesting injustice have effectively employed
nonterrorist measures—dissent, disobedience, and passive resistance. They have also used violence that was not
terroristic, since it was directed against targets themselves
rather than against innocent victims. Revolutionary and
liberationist movements have repudiated terror, as in
Marxist theory and in Ghandi's practice. The defense of
terror as a necessary evil is superficial and groundless.

A more sophisticated defense claims poetic justice: It
is the terrorist who is the innocent victim. The major
premise of this defense is a generalization about prior
wrongs now being redressed. This line of argument was
implied by the United States U.N. Ambassador, Andrew

Young. He countered American expressions of concern for political prisoners in the Soviet Union by referring to the thousands of political prisoners in the United States. Mr. Young explained that he applied the term "political prisoner" to any criminal who was a victim of poverty and discrimination.

In connection with terrorism, the major premise of the poetic justice defense presents the terrorist as a victim of pervasive and unremitting violence; his victims are not innocent because they shared in perpetrating this systematic violence. Violence has been defined as any cause of needless reduction in basic freedoms for any human being. By this definition, poverty and discrimination are indeed forms of violence. So too are ideologies in defense of dictatorship or terror, though the ideologue will claim that neither his ideology nor the reduction in freedom he is espousing is needless.

"It confuses the issue," a critic has pointed out, "to use the emotively loaded word *violence,* when the grievance can be better described and treated under another name; the term 'injustice' also has much emotive force."[4] The sweeping usage, however, gives the ideologue the opportunity to argue that the violence he defends is only a response to violence already inflicted. Poetic justice is guaranteed by the definition.

The theme of counter-violence is developed by Herbert Marcuse with explicit reference to terrorism, and with a claim not only of moral justification for terror but even of a moral obligation to use it. "Terror may become a necessity and an obligation. Here, violence, revolutionary violence, appears not only as a political means but as a moral duty. The terror is defined as counter-violence."[5] The argument is that the target has used violence all along;

to object to terrorism is to hold that the target has a right to use violence but that his victims do not.

"Suppression and sacrifice are daily exacted by all societies," Marcuse continues, "and one cannot start—indeed I would like to say this with all possible emphasis—one cannot start becoming moral and ethical at an arbitrary but expedient point of cutoff: the point of revolution."[6] From his own premises the conclusion might instead be drawn, not that terror is a moral obligation, but that both suppression and terror are immoral. Why not start becoming moral and ethical right now, instead of waiting until after the revolution? Marcuse's retort is that morality is impossible without revolution; the use of terror makes morality also impossible *with* revolution.

Whether the use of terror, as distinguished from other means of redress, is justified remains questionable even when the oppression undeniably exists. But when the oppression is merely alleged, the issue becomes far sharper, especially when that allegation is challenged. Not every national identity, for example, has an acknowledged right to statehood. Multinational states are not *ipso facto* oppressive, certainly not so oppressive as to justify the use of terror against them. Terrorists whose target is Israel are supported because they are aspiring to their "just rights," a political expression of their national identity. The same defense could then be made of terrorism directed against other multinational states: Canada, Britain, Belgium, Spain, Yugoslavia, the Soviet Union, India, and many others. A selective sense of justice makes these reasons suspect as rationalizations.

Rationalization is invoked because realism and rationality cannot countenance the argument that two wrongs make a right. President McKinley's assassin explained, "It is not right that the President should have everything and we should have nothing." His disordered mind could not understand that killing the President does not give "us" something to redress the balance. In the last century, the almighty dollar and gunboat diplomacy were widely condemned. In our time, petrodollars and the politics of terror not only escape condemnation; it is their victims who are condemned, on what purport to be moral grounds.

One sin brings another in its train: First terror is excused, then it is glorified:

> Vice is a monster of so frightful mien,
> As to be hated needs but to be seen;
> Yet seen too oft, familiar with her face,
> We first endure, then pity, then embrace.

That was written in the Age of Reason by Alexander Pope, in his "Essay on Man." To many people today, vice does not look so bad to start with.

With regard to terror, more than familiarity is at work; an ethical variant of the genetic fallacy is applied. The causes of an action are treated as if they were reasons for it, and the reasons, in turn, are taken to be justifications. To understand behavior may require that we suspend moral judgment—but only suspend it, not abandon it. To understand all is not to forgive all, any more than discovering the etiology of a disease makes it any less unwelcome. Those who seek scientific understanding of behavior are not freed by their scientific aim from the obligation to make moral discriminations. Science and morals are not enemies except when pretended morality is irrational and when a presumptuous science puts itself above moral responsibility.

That a brutal crime has its roots in poverty, for example, does not imply that the crime is therefore not brutal after all. On the contrary, this is why we say poverty is brutalizing. The morality of acts of desperation is not determined by what made those who carry out the acts so desperate. Indeed, many terrorists, far from being desperate, belong to the more privileged classes of their societies. The reason terrorists act as they do does not answer the question whether what they do is morally justified.[7]

The glorification of violence in defiance of the moral norms of a civilized tradition was characteristic of fascism. That is why decent men and women around the world found fascism abhorrent. Today the glorification of violence has been taken up by self-styled progressives and revolutionaries. A new romanticism has made heroes of the virtuosos of violence. The rhetoric of the apostles of terror is hardly new. Shakespeare has Brutus exclaim after the assassination of Caesar,

> . . . waving our red weapons o'er our heads,
> Let's all cry, peace, freedom, and liberty!

to which Cassius adds,

> . . . How many ages hence,
> Shall this our lofty scene be acted over,
> In states unborn, and accents yet unknown!

We have a duty to call things by their right names. Political motives do not automatically transform murderers into freedom fighters or guerillas. The pretense of terrorists to the legitimacy of military action would sometimes be comic were it not for its tragic outcomes. When a class of school children was held captive by terrorists in Ma'alot, "military communiques" were issued with unconscious and grisly humor; twenty-seven children were killed in this "military" operation.

It is moral blindness to give the name *guerilla* to those whose sphere of action is not military installations or locales of even indirect military significance—like bridges, railroads, and factories—but rather civilian airports, markets, city streets, bus stops, and bathing beaches, to say nothing of schoolrooms, apartment houses, and rest homes. The act of terror displays only cowardice; seldom do these "heroes" attack anyone other than unarmed civilians.

Making heroes of terrorists is reminiscent of the former glamorization of gangsters and the outlaws of the Old West. Children have played cops-and-robbers for untold generations; no doubt such fantasies have a constructive element. Maturity, as well as morality, requires that they remain fantasies and not be acted out.

On the borderline of psychopathology, or perhaps over the border, is a certain pornography of violence widespread in our time. I am not referring here to out-and-out sadism, though there may be more in common between sadists like the Manson family and terrorists like the Baader-Meinhof gang than ideologues care to face. I am referring to the perception of violence, especially of terrorism, as an expression of *machismo;* the readiness to kill is seen as a mark of virility. Perversion glamorizes the female terrorist as well: Her crossed gunbelts are displayed to project an image akin to high boots and whip.

Hero or no, the terrorist today is unquestionably a celebrity. Terrorism, to a significant degree, is a product of the mass media, and might not survive without the media. The terrorist act must have an audience, or who will be terrorized? The terrorist group must maintain a high profile, or who will fear them? Public opinion must be mobilized in support of the terrorist aims, rival groups must be impressed, and potential sources of support must be won over and kept content.

The media have special obligations in covering terror as they do with regard to other events like sex crimes and juvenile offenses. Their coverage, especially during the terrorist action but afterwards too, must be severely restricted, so as not to exacerbate the situation in process, nor to intensify afterwards the gains terrorists can expect from further terrorist acts. Targets of terror have a similar obligation to deflate both the terrorist and his activity; public responses by high government officials serve the terrorists' aims whatever the content of the responses might be. In terror, the medium *is* the message.

Responses to terror raise other ethical considerations. Negotiating with terrorists (instead of calling for their surrender) implies a relationship between equals that cannot be morally countenanced, unless one views terrorism as morally acceptable. In such negotiations the terrorist is given privileges ordinarily denied to law-abiding citizens, privileges like access to important officials and to the mass media. Honoring agreements reached with terrorists overlooks the glaring circumstance that the agreements were coerced, and so have no moral or legal validity. To keep faith with terrorists is to strengthen faith in terror.

Many ideologues, in and out of government, advocate responses to terror in accord with an "even-handed, balanced" policy. The act of terror is equated with action taken to defend against it or to deter it; both forms of violence are then righteously deplored. In this perspective the terrorist is a political idealist actuated by unselfish aims, and is not wholly to blame. This is an easy view for apologists in nations not under terrorist attack. To the victim of terror this approach conveys the attitude that the tiger is only seeking food after all, and since his prey has four limbs, in all fairness he should be willing to part with one or two.

The policy of even-handedness springs less from a sense of justice—not a conspicuous virtue of governments—than from venality and political cowardice. This conclusion is reinforced by the frequency with which captured terrorists are released without being brought to trial, or, if convicted, are made to serve only a small fraction of their sentences. "The one means that wins the easiest victory over reason," a political writer has maintained, "is terror and force." The writer is Adolf Hitler.[8] When economic pressures—not only oil but also billions of dollars in purchasing power—are also at work, the victory is virtually assured.

The underlying ethical issue is whether a political motive gives terror a moral standing it would otherwise lack. Apologists for terror hold that assassination is not murder, taking hostages is not kidnapping, hijacking is not piracy. The Geneva Convention on the High Seas (1958), a convention that applies also to aircraft, in its definition of piracy explicitly exempts acts not committed "for private ends." Given such a frame of reference, political terror must be assessed on a political basis only, not a moral or a legal basis. At any rate, the political motive is thought to be an important mitigating circumstance.

Motives are significant for understanding what action has been performed and why. But motives enter into moral assessment only by way of the consequences that would flow in the long run from acts so motivated and carried out in such circumstances. The pardoning of well-intentioned acts usually rests on examination of but a restricted

set of consequences. An embezzler who distributes his ac-
quisitions in private philanthropies is still a thief. Who
benefits by his charity must be weighed against who is
robbed—not only of the fruits of their labor but, as in the
case of hostages, of their freedom. The road to hell is paved
with good intentions.

The political terrorist is usually not acting singly, or as
part of a small conspiracy, but (at least in his own eyes) as
the instrument of a broad political movement. It is a terrorist group that claims responsibility for terrorist action;
the individual terrorist claims to be exempt from responsibility. One of the most perplexing moral problems of our
time is that while action is increasingly corporate, only
individuals can be held morally accountable.

Martin Buber argued that what is wrong for the individual cannot be right for the group, a statement that goes
too far. It is wrong for one individual to extort money from
another but a state may collect taxes; it is wrong for one
individual to use force to compel another but a state may
rightfully exercise police power. The immorality of terror
does not lie in the assertion that a group is doing something that an individual may not do. Terrorists employ code
names not as a security measure, since the names are
openly published, but rather to mark the terrorist's group
identity, by which he is absolved of personal responsibility.

Even though an individual acts in the name of a group,
however, it is always he himself who is morally responsible. This is the doctrine formulated in the Nuremburg
trials: "Crimes against international law are committed by
men, not by abstract entities, and only by punishing individuals who commit such crimes can the provisions of
international law be enforced."[9] The United Nations Gen-

eral Assembly, though today unwilling to outlaw terrorism, reaffirmed the principles of Nuremburg by a resolution of November 21, 1947.

Not every individual is equally responsible for every action of the state or society. That is the assumption terrorists sometimes make, to prove that there are no innocent victims because everyone is responsible for the grievances the terrorists seek to redress. But an individual is responsible only to the extent of his individual impact on the group's actions. One who freely joins a terrorist group and volunteers for a terrorist mission is wholly responsible. Brainwashing or other subtle forms of coercion (as in the case of Patty Hearst) may lessen that responsibility. A functionary carrying out orders may be less responsible than those who give the orders, though he is not altogether free of responsibility, as is a citizen who dissents from policies he abhors. In short, individual terrorists, not abstract political entities, are morally accountable.

The morality of the individual terrorist hinges on the ethics of *absolutism*. In absolutism certain ends of action are assigned an absolute value and are considered worth pursuing no matter what the consequences. The 19th century Russian anarchist Mikhail Bakunin formulated a political example: "Whatever aids the triumph of revolution is ethical; all that hinders it is unethical and criminal." Contemporary absolutisms may replace "revolution" by national liberation. Marcuse points to the destructiveness of religious absolutism: "As long as a transcendent sanction of ethics was accepted . . . infidels could justly be exterminated, heretics could justly be burned."[10] He does not note that "historical necessity" and "national interest" may make equally deadly claims. Political doctrine is invoked to justify extermination just as is religious doctrine.

Religion and politics can unite to form especially unyielding absolutisms, as in several of the Islamic dictatorships.

Sidney Hook has tellingly criticized the absolutism of conscience that "ritualistic liberals" substituted for the absolutism of law, especially in the protest movements of a decade ago.[11] Disobedience of any law that runs counter to conscience is a principle that, if unqualified, negates the rule of law, for conscience notoriously varies from person to person. If conscience is God-given, it is, in Freud's words, "a careless and uneven piece of work." The tyranny of conscience has claimed more victims by far than has merely unprincipled opportunism. The fact that the terrorist is driven by a conviction that he is claiming his "just rights" does not automatically endow his acts of terror with moral justification.

The besetting sin of the absolutist is a total lack of humility; he is utterly incapable of asking himself, "And what if I am wrong?" He mistakes himself for God's vicar on earth, and his private fantasies of the good for a vision of Paradise. To acknowledge a margin for error need not sap the springs of action. What it does is to invite deliberation on the consequences of planned action and assessment of the projected ends on the basis of the means they call for. Not all action is threatened by taking thought, only such action as scuttles for cover from the light of reason. Absolutism, like other forms of irrationality, is self-defeating. When we say, "Let justice be done though the heavens fall," they do fall, and justice lies broken in the ruins.

Absolutism founders on the bitter truth that the means we employ shape our ends. The pursuit itself colors the worth of the pursued; the pursuit becomes part of the pursued's substance. To say of the terrorist, "I sympathize with his ends, though I disapprove of his means" expresses the same naïveté that would say of the rapist, "He only wants love." The Deuteronomist's injunction, "Justice, justice shalt thou pursue!" repeats the word justice, commentators explain, because if there is no justice in our pursuits there will be no justice in our attainments.

Morality is at one with the law in holding that whoever wills to use specific means is willing the ends that reasonably are to be expected from those means. That is why absolutism is self-defeating. "There are forms of violence and suppression which no revolutionary situation can justify," Marcuse acknowledges, "because they negate the very end for which the revolution is a means. Such are arbitrary violence, cruelty, and indiscriminate terror."[12] Terror by its very nature is arbitrary, cruel, and indiscriminate. The terrorist is indifferent to the identity of his victims, and knows that the more cruel his act, the greater the terror it inspires.

Morality, in weighing the consequences of action, looks particularly to effects on character, on life-style, on the quality of life. He that lives by the sword dies by the sword, not because cosmic powers are bent on punishing him, but because the swordsman is, at the last, unable to lay down his weapon. The vulgar pragmatism that worships success grossly distorts the philosophic doctrine, by being blind to the price success exacts. A terrorist like Idi Amin may become head of the Organization of African Unity, and a terrorist like Yasser Arafat may be acclaimed in the General Assembly of the United Nations; morality condemns them both, for all that.

The dissociation of ends from means is embodied in the *fallacy of absolute priority:* first I will get rich, then live a life of leisurely contemplation; first I will win office, then govern justly; first I will attain power, then promulgate peace and freedom. The terrorist's version of the Gospels teaches, "Seek ye first the kingdom of this earth, and all these things shall be added unto you." But that day never comes.

The latent contradiction between immoral means and noble ends is manifest in expressions like Robespierre's "despotism of liberty." His Reign of Terror did not bring liberty, equality, and fraternity; the king was guillotined only to be replaced by an emperor. In the "dictatorship of the proletariat" it is easy to identify the dictators; as for the proletariat, it is just as easy to see a "needless reduction in its basic freedoms." A "secular, democratic state" in Palestine is still being called for by the bloc whose members are as secular as Libya and Iran, and as democratic as Saudia Arabia and Iraq.

It has been conjectured that, psychologically, the terrorist is seeking to regain a paradise lost.[13] What he does is very real; what he hopes for remains fantasy. "Radicals" and "urban guerillas" in the United States, Italy, West Germany, and Japan suppose that bombing banks and shooting down corporation executives will replace capitalism with a more humane society. In fact, these acts do not make way for the new order, but merely destroy individual victims. Terrorists have been called "revolutionists in a hurry"; the truth is that "terrorism has tended to retard rather than advance the cause of social reform. The victims of the assassins are easily replaced; a regime . . . is galvanized into action; and all reformers are plausibly stigmatized."[14]

The terrorist has committed himself to prophecy: He justifies what he does by predicting the future he is bringing about—a future so probable and so much more desirable than the present as to make the act of terror worth-while. He relies on what Marcuse calls a "historical calculus"—the "calculation of the chances of a future society as against the chances of the existing society with respect to human progress."[15] Marcuse acknowledges that such a calculus is "inhumane" and even "brutal"; it must nevertheless be applied, because the calculus is not "an empty intellectual abstraction; in fact, at its decisive turns, history became such a calculated experiment." There is a missing premise in this logic: Hegel's principle that whatever is, is right. Only a tortuous dialectic can provide the needed rationalization.

In Marcuse's justification of counter-violence the shoe is on the other foot: "Who can quantify and who can compare the sacrifices exacted by an established society and those exacted by its subversion?"[16] But if quantifications and comparisons cannot be made, what justifies terrorist violence? It is hard enough to predict the outcome of rational action; "those who would predict the outcome of violence are brash indeed."[17] When blood is spilled for the sake of such uncertain futures, pretended idealism is unmasked as savagery. All that can be predicted of violence is that if it is not resisted it will continue to claim its victims.

The destruction that terror wreaks is sure, while its goals are visionary and doubtful. Taking such a risk is hardly grounded in rational realistic expectations; the inference that other motivations are at work is ineluctable. The terrorist does not turn to violence merely as a means to his ends—for him, it is an end in itself. The mugger typically beats his victim after robbing him; he robs to have occasion for the beating. The rapist is filled, not with lust, but with anger and hate. Widespread today is a cult of violence, complete with sacrifices, priesthood, and theologians.

Violence is glorified in our time as poverty was glorified in another age: It builds character, and is the cradle of all the virtues. "Irrepressible violence is man recreating himself," Sartre has said, ". . . through mad fury the wretched of the earth become men."[18] An infantile belief in the magic of violence has become pandemic: the belief that any action, if it is violent enough, is bound to succeed.

There is no need to trace causal connections or to deliberate on conditions and consequences. We pound the malfunctioning television set, kick the Coke machine, practice lobotomies, engage in saturation bombing, and carry out acts of terror.

There are many ways to resolve conflicts, violence being but the final recourse. The cult of violence, though, gives force unchallenged priority in the political arena. "The first maxim of our policy," said Robespierre, "should be to conduct the people by reason, and the enemies of the people by terror." The irony is that only the so-called enemies of the people are ready to negotiate; terrorism has no use for talk. Frequent targets of violence linked to terrorist action are the mediators of nonviolent conflict resolution: law makers, judges, election officials. It has become a cliché of our time that law and morality live in the barrel of a rifle, provided the police are not wielding it.

The ethics I am articulating do not condemn every use of force; pacifism may also be immoral. There is a moral obligation, after all, to struggle against injustice. Turning the other cheek is seldom an effective device for changing another's behavior. But ethics do condemn violence for its own sake, the same violence that claims innocent victims—in a word, terror. In this world of fenced-in frontiers, the guns, it has been said, point in the direction of freedom. Terror provides another significant signpost of the direction of freedom. Terror manifests the politics of hate. Who are the haters and who is the hated is a touchstone of political morality.

Surrender to terror is moral as well as political cowardice. The rationale that to surrender is only to save lives disregards all the future lives put at stake when terrorism is allowed to succeed. "To be tough on terrorists," the surrender argument runs, "turns out to be tough on the victims." But to surrender *is* eventually tough on the victims—and tough on everyone else at the same time. For rewarding an action can only encourage its repitition.

The terrorist argues that if we do not meet his demands it is we who are responsible for the fate of hostages. To accept this allocation of responsibility is to abandon both law and morality. It would brand the police criminals, and leave the law-abiding with blood on their hands.

A "policy of flexibility" announces to the terrorist that he has chances of success, and heightens his expectation of at least moderate gains. Such flexibility applied to other crimes would mean that we'd let bank-robbers rob a bank once in a while, arsonists light a fire on occasion, and rapists rape a woman now and then—all only under special circumstances, of course. Moral integrity is not a species of absolutism; it means acting on our moral principles, not merely making pious declarations afterwards.

Criminologists agree that the most effective deterrent

to crime is swift and sure punishment. The release of captured terrorists doubly violates morality. It is unjust to those guilty of lesser offenses, and encourages terrorism.

Even the perpetrator of such an unequivocal outrage as the murder of the Olympic athletes in Munich was released by France. These criminals are often extradited to countries that forego even the pretense of mock trials; conditions of release are cynically disregarded even by men of the cloth such as Archbishop Capucci. Such a climate of world opinion makes raising moral issues almost pointless.

Where moral sensibilities have not been altogether blunted, demands for capital punishment of terrorists are often heard. Such executions might meet inner needs; but they cannot be justified on the basis of external consequences. Years of capital punishment in dozens of jurisdictions have failed to provide convincing evidence of its deterrent effect. To take a human life deliberately, whether of a terrorist or of anyone else, only because we think it might produce a desired result, is to be guilty of the same immorality condemned in the act of terror. Capital punishment may even encourage terrorism, for if the terrorist is performing a sacrament of violence, his own death is but the symbolic fulfillment of his life.[19]

A deterrent as effective as swift and sure punishment of the terrorist is punishment of the "accessories"—governments that, before and after the fact, train and offer refuge to terrorist groups. Many nations have readily submitted to boycotts as a sanction. But these boycotts have been imposed for political ends; an international consensus on using boycotts to enforce moral standards seems far in the future.

In 1820 the pirate was declared an enemy of the human race, even though piracy in the form of privateering had served for some time as a political instrument. A hundred years later, moves to suppress terrorism were widespread among those concerned with maintaining the international legal order. Between the world wars such efforts intensified, only to be thwarted in recent decades by the alliance between the Communist and Arab blocs. Efforts today are sporadic and half-hearted, except in those countries that have been targets of terrorism.

Those who mold opinion in the democratic countries—intellectuals, clergy, and others—have failed to take a strong moral stand, because they have split politically on this issue. But the issue is moral, not political. "Terror commits its deepest injury," a philosophical sociologist has remarked, "when it tempts us to silence."[20] It may be committing a deeper injury when it induces ideologues to speak out in defense of terror. They do so because they are identifying with the terrorist rather than with his victims. The victims themselves (if they survive) characteristically speak well of terrorists, out of identification with the aggressor. Ideological identification is harder to explain.

Some years ago I was a delegate to a White House conference on youth and heard a young man argue down a motion to condemn terrorism, on the grounds that "you can't make an omelet without breaking eggs." He was quoting Robespierre's excuse for the Reign of Terror. In my ears it was a particularly lame excuse, for I had just returned from the Galilee, where a school bus had been machine-gunned by terrorists a few days before. My conviction was irresistible that had he been sitting in the bus along with the other youngsters, such an argument would have filled him with horror.

"Do not stand idly by the blood of your fellows," Scripture enjoins. When the blood is your own, morality coincides with simple self-interest, and duty with natural impulse. If terror is allowed to flourish anywhere, men everywhere are condemned to live in fear.

REFERENCES

1. Rubinoff ML: Violence and retreat from reason. In *Reason and Violence*. Edited by Stanage SM. Totowa, New Jersey: Littlefield Adams, 1974, p 76.
2. Blanshard B: Morality and politics. In *Ethics and Society*. Edited by DeGeorge R. Garden City, New York: Anchor Doubleday, 1966, p 1.
3. Blackstone W: *Commentaries*, vol 4, p 27.
4. Audi R: Violence, legal sanctions, and law enforcement. In *Reason and Violence*. Edited by Stanage SM. Totowa, New Jersey: Littlefield Adams, 1974, p 37.
5. Marcuse H: Ethics and revolution. In *Ethics and Society*. Edited by DeGeorge R. Garden City, New Jersey: Anchor Doubleday, 1966, p 37.
6. Ibid, p 145.
7. Kaplan A: The psychodynamics of terrorism. *Terrorism: An International Journal* 1:237–238, 1978.
8. Hitler A: Chapter 2 of *Mein Kampf*, vol 1. Hollywood, California: Angriff Press, 1962.
9. *International Military Tribunal 1947–1949*, vol 1. New York: AMS Press, p 223.
10. Marcuse H: Ethics and revolution. In *Ethics and Society*. Edited by DeGeorge R. Garden City, New Jersey: Anchor Doubleday, 1966, p 142.
11. Hook S: Social protest and civil disobedience. In *Moral Problems in Contemporary Society*. Edited by Kurtz P. Englewood Cliffs, New Jersey: Prentice-Hall, 1969, p 166.

12. Marcuse H: Ethics and revolution. In *Ethics and Society.* Edited by DeGeorge R. Garden City, New Jersey: Anchor Doubleday, 1966, p 141.
13. Van den Haag E: *Political Violence and Civil Disobedience.* New York: Harper & Row, 1972, p 88.
14. Girvetz H: An anatomy of violence. In *Reason and Violence.* Edited by Stanage SM. Totowa, New Jersey: Littlefield Adams, 1974, p 191.
15. Marcuse H: Ethics and revolution. In *Ethics and Society.* Edited by DeGeorge R. Garden City, New Jersey: Anchor Doubleday, 1966, p 140.
16. Ibid. p 145.
17. Girvetz H: An anatomy of violence. In *Reason and Violence.* Edited by Stanage SM. Totowa, New Jersey: Littlefield Adams, 1974, p 202.
18. Ibid. p 193.
19. Kaplan A: The psychodynamics of terrorism. *Terrorism: An International Journal* 1:251–252, 1978.
20. O'Neill J: Violence, technology and the body politic. In *Reason and Violence.* Edited by Stanage SM. Totowa, New Jersey: Littlefield Adams, 1974, p 6.

2

The Psychiatrist and the Terrorist*

JOHN GUNN, M.D.†

It is with some diffidence that I discuss the subject of terrorism, since my working knowledge of hijacking, sieges, and other activities related to terrorism is confined to information gleaned from newspapers, scientific articles, books, and discussions with colleagues. Nonetheless, I believe it is profitable to examine some basic principles of relating a medical speciality such as psychiatry to terrorism before others consider in detail the practical issues of direct intervention. In "The Psychiatry of Kidnapping and Hostage Taking," Scott discussed several categories of individuals who have kid-

*This paper is presented essentially as was read at the Baltimore symposium in 1979.
†I would like to thank Paul Bowden, M.D., and Pamela Taylor, M.D., for their very helpful criticism and Frank Ochberg, M.D., who introduced me to this important topic. Maureen Bartholomew and Celia Gunn performed the vital secretarial work that made this chapter possible.

napped or taken hostages: the lone operators, both rational and irrational; the group operators, irrational; the professional criminals, seeking either money or escape; and the politically motivated terrorist.[1] This chapter concerns the last category only, the politically motivated terrorist, who is rational in his or her objectives and usually operates as a member of a group.

Before discussing the ethics of an association between psychiatry and political terrorists, we must consider some general issues in medical ethics. It is also important to emphasize that ethics are not sets of rules or an agreed code. Clearly, ethical codes are often established, but ethics is the branch of philosophy in which moral questions are debated.

Furthermore, ethical ideas are not immutable and static; they change as culture and mores change, and are influenced by new technologies and new problems. Ethical questions are raised by conflicts, by opposing interests, and by ideas. Moreover, I want to suggest, along with Clouser,[2] that some debates are not simply about moral issues; they also involve matters of taste and personal preference. A given circumstance may elicit several possible actions, none of which breaks a moral rule; alternatively, some or all of these reactions may infringe upon one another. An example is the controversy over the wearing of seat belts. Valid ethical arguments can be espoused both for requiring all motorists to wear belts, and for leaving the decision to the individual. I know this controversy quite well and have changed sides in the past few years, using ethical arguments to support each position in turn. In fact, I have used economic, aesthetic, and other grounds in making my final decision.

MEDICAL ETHICS

Most observers consider medical ethics to have their root in the Hippocratic oath, probably written around 370 B.C. As Moore suggests,[3] the oath has two basic parts:

> The first is a sworn covenant for the physician to honour his teacher as a parent and to teach his teacher's sons by the same sworn covenant. . . . The second part of the Hippocratic oath is a series of rules that are familiar to us today, a true code of ethics, including such items as protecting patient confidentiality, avoiding sexual contact, performing no surgery, and protecting the patient from harm.

Blomquist pointed out that this pagan code became Christianized about 1,000 years ago, largely because the Hippocratic ethics are compatible with Christian ethics, even though the former were isolationist, individualistic, and paternalistic. He likened the medical fraternity to a priesthood that has to accept certain articles of faith and protect that faith from outside contamination. However, he pointed out that modern belief in empirical research and in informed consent challenges the paternalistic view of medicine as we give increasing weight to scientific knowledge, public education, and free choice, and place less emphasis on the special powers of the professional.[4]

Currently the basic code of ethics for all physicians is the 1948 Declaration of Geneva as amended in 1968:

> As a member of the medical profession:
>
> I solemnly pledge myself to consecrate my life to the service of humanity.
>
> I will give to my teachers the respect and gratitude which are their due.

I will practice my profession with conscience and dignity.

The health of my patient will be my first consideration.

I will respect the secrets which are confided in me.

I will maintain by all the means of my power the honour and the noble traditions of the medical profession.

My colleagues will be my brothers.

I will not permit considerations of religion, nationality, race, party politics, or social standing to intervene between my duty and my patient.

I will maintain the utmost respect for human life from the time of conception; even under threat, I will not use my medical knowledge contrary to the law of humanity.

This code is a direct descendant of the Hippocratic tradition, and although its first clause is a pledge to humanity, its main emphasis is on the individual patient rather than the community in general. Blomquist argues correctly that the difficulty with codes of medical ethics is that physicians have multiple loyalties and that total loyalty to the patient is neither possible nor a good ethic.[4] Doctors are well aware of the conflicts that can arise when patients' interests diverge from the interests of the community. A classic situation arises when an epileptic patient refuses to tell the authorities of his disability because he knows they will revoke his driver's license and insists that his physician also keep the information confidential. Very few doctors will put the patient's request above the community interest in this case. Some will simply say, "Unless you tell the authorities, I will discharge you from my care." Others will go so far as to tell the authorities despite the patient's objections.

There are two reasons for these decisions. First, it simply is not in the long-term interest of the patient to collude with his illegal acts. He may be injured or killed by suffering a seizure while driving—a paternalistic and not too impressive reason. Unless there are good grounds for regarding a patient as having reduced responsibility for his actions (for example mental deficiency or mental illness), then the most a physician should do about health hazards is to spell out the best available advice very clearly.

The second reason appears more valid. If a particular policy is adopted, the doctor must balance the advantages and disadvantages to the patient against the advantages and disadvantages to the community. In that balancing act, he must also decide whether he is prepared to go as far as breaking the law himself in carrying out his patient's requests. In the example above, the disadvantages of collusion with the patient include a possibly fatal road accident involving others as well as the patient. Similar disadvantages to the public arise when it seems likely that the release of a forensic patient who has insight and a reasonable measure of responsibility for his own actions may result in harm or death to a number of other individuals. The dilemmas are more difficult because predictions are very inexact and harm to the patient by prolonged incarceration may be considerable. Nonetheless, the ethical process of balancing interests has to be the same. One practical technique that can be helpful in this situation is to have more than one individual involved in making the decision, one of the practitioners being clearly identified with the patient and arguing the patient's case as an advocate.

In response to the expanding disciplines of medicine, separate codes have been developed for aspects of medical work that are not primarily directed to patients. For example, the 1964 Declaration of Helsinki guides medical researchers. I am not aware, however, of any international principles that guide physicians in their role as advisors to organizations. At first thought such a code may not seem essential, but clearly a doctor working for an organization could face a conflict of interest. To take a hypothetical example: I am an industrial medical officer working for a firm producing a noxious chemical. I suspect that the chemical may be endangering the long-term health of some of the employees. Is my first responsibility to the firm that employs me or to each individual employee? Almost certainly my first communication will be with the employer, who pays my salary, but I expect overriding medical ethics would prevent me from colluding with any commercial interest against the interests of the employees. In other words, I am quite sure that for such circumstances a code of practice could be established to conform with general social ethics, the basic responsibility of employee to employer, and the general principles of medical ethics.

Other organizations may pose different problems for doctors they employ. For example, prison doctors sometimes face the following conflict of interest: Is a physician acting in the patient's best interest when certifying him fit for punishment? Again, to my knowledge, no special code of ethics for this situation has been developed, although discussion has started in the British literature.[5] More recently, Ochberg and I have discussed the problems that confront a doctor employed by a police authority.[6]

PSYCHIATRIC ETHICS

Psychiatry, as a central branch of medicine, has the same ethical framework as any other speciality. There are, however, one or two additional problems. A significant one is the issue of making recommendations for involuntary commitment and for release. In 1977, the general assembly of the World Psychiatric Association, in response to questions on the compulsory treatment of political dissenters, established a series of guidelines for psychiatrists in the Declaration of Hawaii.[7] It embodies ten fairly detailed clauses. Not all the clauses are relevant here, but some are worth quoting:

i. The aim of psychiatry is to promote health and personal autonomy and growth. To the best of his or her ability, consistent with accepted scientific and ethical principles, the psychiatrist shall serve the best interests of the patient and be also concerned for the common good and a just allocation of health resources.

iii. A therapeutic relationship between patient and psychiatrist is founded on mutual agreement. It requires trust, confidentiality, openness, co-operation, and mutual responsibility. Such a relationship may not be possible with some severely ill patients. In that case, as in the treatment of children, contact should be established with a person close to the patient and acceptable to him or her.

If and when a relationship is established for purposes other than therapeutic ones, such as in forensic psychiatry, its nature must be thoroughly explained to the person concerned.

v. No procedure must be performed or treatment given against or independent of a patient's own will, unless the patient lacks capacity to express his or her own wishes or, owing to psychiatric illness, cannot see what is in his or her best interests or, for the same reason, is a severe threat to others. In these cases compulsory treatment may or should be given, provided that it is done in the patient's best interests and over a reasonable period of time a retroactive informed consent may be presumed, and, whenever possible, consent has been obtained from someone close to the patient.

vii. The psychiatrist must never use the possibilities of the profession for maltreatment of individuals or groups, and should be concerned never to let inappropriate personal desires, feelings, or prejudices interfere with the treatment.

The psychiatrist must not participate in compulsory psychiatric treatment in the absence of psychiatric illness. If the patient or some third party demands actions contrary to scientific or ethical principles the psychiatrist must refuse to co-operate. When, for any reason, either the wishes or the best interest of the patient cannot be promoted he or she must be so informed.

Quite clearly the code faces the problem that psychiatrists are sometimes in a paternalistic even custodial role when their patients' personal interests are not the only consideration. Moreover, it recognizes, in its first clause, that the psychiatrist shall be "concerned for the common good."

How far psychiatry should travel down the road of "common good" and concern itself with social questions is a matter of debate. Curran,[8] Lewis,[9] Miller,[10] and Shepherd[11] have all argued for a limited role for psychiatry. Miller's view is the most trenchant:

The Oxford Dictionary's definition of a psychiatrist is "one who treats mental disease." Not, you will observe, one who prevents wars, cures anti-semitism, offers to transform the normally abrasive relations between men into a tedium of stultifying harmony, is the ultimate authority on bringing up children or selecting directors, or misuses his jargon to confuse any and every topical issue in an incessant series of television appearances.

However, in a survey conducted by the Task Force on Intervening in Community Crises, 50 percent of the APA respondents said they would be willing to be trained to function in community crises, such as racial conflicts and campus disputes, and 12 percent said they have been specially trained in social crisis intervention.[12]

I think it is premature to rigidly define the psychiatrist's role in society, but surely a balance must be reached between the belief that medical practitioners should confine their concern to medical matters, and the belief that they can play a magical, omniscient role in resolving complex social problems. This latter belief stems, at least in part, from the understandable desire for magicians during a crisis, a role played by medicine men in more primitive societies. But medicine men relieve anxiety, partly by accepting responsibility for resolving the crisis.

Ultimately, of course, the psychiatrist's role will be influenced by public pressure, since the doctor is in one sense a public servant. But the medical profession will always want to temper this public pressure with its own ethics and scientific findings. In my view, doctors should espouse only those skills they actually possess, and make health matters their prime concern. Certainly in the course of their careers psychiatrists acquire a good deal of psychological insight. But they may still lack the training to apply this insight to practical problems.

For example, it has been suggested that because psychiatrists conduct therapeutic assessment interviews, they may make good negotiators in a siege. This assumption strikes me as naïve. Trade union officials, police, and other professionals have been specifically trained for this kind of work and are much more well versed in the tactics of negotiating.

HEALTH ETHICS

When the World Health Organization (WHO) advised the United Nations about the health aspects of the avoidable maltreatment of prisoners and detainees, it drew a clear distinction between medical ethics and health ethics.[13] The former were defined as "the unwritten rules of personal conduct governing the professional relationships of physicians with their patients or with each other." These ethics, actually rules of conduct, are to be left to the World Medical Association to devise. The organization pointed out that its contribution made no mention of ethics, even by implication.

Even so, the organization has taken upon itself a concern in what it calls "health ethics," which it defines as the accountability of governments to their populations in regard to health matters. The World Health Organization Constitution contains a single objective: "the attainment by all peoples of the highest possible level of health." The conclusion is that member governments are under an obligation to do what is in their power to protect their citizens from avoidable hazards to physical or mental health, and to ensure access to medical care. "It follows," so the argument runs, "that WHO and its constituent governments must necessarily be opposed to any procedures that offer a deliberate threat to physical or mental health, whether such procedures are undertaken with or without the active or passive connivance of physicians or members of any other health profession." This statement clearly indicates that all government employees should concern themselves with the health of *all* citizens, a position not dissimilar to a doctor's. Such a code must apply to police officers and other law-keepers, especially during sieges, so perhaps the gap between police officer and psychiatrist need not be as great as might first appear.

THE PSYCHIATRIST AND THE POLICE

Increasingly, psychiatrists are asked to advise the police. In general, physicians do not regard police work as incompatible with their ordinary role of caring for patients. In most psychiatrists, though, such requests give rise to immediate anxiety. For psychiatrists, there is always the suspicion that they are being called to advise about controlling behavior—control that could lead to social repression. Of course, psychiatry is concerned to some degree with social control. And some believe that psychiatrists, more than other professionals, have special skills that enable them to control the behavior of others. Personally, I think that outside the clinical situation this belief is largely mythical and is related to the medicine man fantasies I mentioned earlier. But I do concede there is a possibility that over time such techniques could be developed.

But the most important problem is the fairly obvious difference in role between police officer and psychiatrist. Traditional medical ethics strongly emphasize patient interests first and community interests a very poor second. For the police officer, these priorities are reversed.

In our earlier paper Ochberg and I discussed how psychiatrists work with the police.[6] Psychiatrists train them to understand more about mental health. Psychiatrists, as medical scientists, research the mental health aspects and effects of policework. Psychiatrists collaborate with police officers when problems involving overt mental illness are encountered, such as when a patient threatens someone's life, attempts suicide, or runs amok. We acknowledged our debt to the police, who are indispensable to work with dangerous patients in specialized clinics such as drug addiction services or emergency rooms, or in practices treating patients with problems of impulse control and aggressive behavior.

In the paper, we focused on five important issues that stem from the interaction of psychiatry and police work. First, we suggested both police and psychiatrists should scrupulously maintain their respective identities. Second, in accepting the distinction, drawn by WHO, between health ethics and medical ethics, we suggested that these health ethics should be more widely discussed. Third, we expressed concern about patient information collected for one purpose and then used for an entirely different purpose. The potential for this is great when psychiatrists and police collaborate. Psychiatrists should take care about discussing patient data. Fourth, we suggested that peer review plays an important part in this kind of work. Doctors working with police agencies should constantly invite the advice and criticism of their medical colleagues. Only through such discussions with peers will physicians ensure that they not become something other than a medical specialist, and that their ethical standards stay in step with those of the rest of the profession. Finally, we stressed that psychiatrists need broader and better education in deontology, the ethics of duty.

I believe that these five issues are particularly relevant to psychiatry's role in solving the problems of terrorism. Without doubt these issues should oversee any work undertaken by psychiatrists in relation to terrorist threats.

Cohen and associates have also discussed some of the issues raised by police-psychiatrist collaboration.[14] They asked ten questions:

1. What are the potential risks and liabilities of working with the police?
2. What do you as a psychiatrist expect to contribute?
3. Have you communicated your expectations?
4. Will your personal values get in the way?

5. What are your preconceptions about the police/psychiatrist relationship?
6. What skills do you bring?
7. What effect will all this have on others not directly involved with the work?
8. To whom are you accountable?
9. How do you assess your effectiveness?
10. Have you communicated the limitations of your skills and services?

These important questions should guide all psychiatrists working with police—particularly those psychiatrists involved in terrorist or siege situations.

THE PSYCHIATRIST AND THE SIEGE

After a long, tortuous, but necessary preamble through general ethical problems in medicine, we come now to specifics. The first question is: Should the psychiatrist be involved with terrorism at all? From one viewpoint, a siege poses health problems to the community in the broadest sense—the very lives of individuals including hostages may be threatened. Therefore, the medical profession should take an interest in the subject.

I agree with this view. But doctors should concentrate on the health issues and, so far as possible, avoid speculating on the sociology, psychology, and politics involved. These areas should be left to academicians and practitioners who have special expertise to offer.

But one just cannot assume that professionals would automatically endorse suppressing all terrorism. After all, the resistance groups that opposed the Nazis during the Second World War were terrorists. And professionals cannot be expected to just blindly obey whatever government is in power. Sometimes higher moral considerations transcend national loyalties. Surely the Nuremberg trials taught this lesson well.

The first point that should be emphasized, therefore, is that a doctor working with a police force fighting a group of terrorists has a role similar to that of a doctor working with any state institutional group. The physician can actively collaborate with the police, thus approving their actions. Or the physican can question the very basis of the police work either by refusing to collaborate at all in a particular instance, or by refusing to collaborate if certain sorts of unacceptable procedures are used. I believe that on one level state authorities and senior police officers welcome the presence of a medical practitioner, who can act as a moral interpreter or a form of conscience. If this is the case, then it is even more important that the doctor be prepared to comment upon and refuse to collaborate with police methods that contravene basic health ethics. This is on an exact par with a doctor's obligation to refuse to collaborate with torture. For example, a doctor might advise against using highly toxic nerve gas to end a siege and then refuse to collaborate further if this advice is ignored.

Given this rather basic proviso, let us see how one or two of the Cohen et al. questions can be applied to the issues considered here.

What Do You Expect to Contribute?

P. D. Scott, the British psychiatrist involved in two London sieges, said clearly

> the task of the psychiatrist in these incidents is secondary to that of the police. He should be unobtrusively there to

give advice when needed. He has a very important part to play in assessing what sort of persons are involved, and advising the negotiator accordingly. He must try to maintain both terrorists and hostages in as good a state of health as possible. . . . A further important function is participating in training programmes to increase the effectiveness of teamwork in the future.[1]

What Skills Do You Bring to the Relationship?

As I have already indicated, I believe that very few psychiatric skills are directly applicable to managing a terrorist siege. Let me re-emphasize that I am not convinced that psychiatrists have any particular expertise as negotiators. Furthermore, I think it would be unethical for a doctor to use the special privileges of the doctor/patient relationship to deceive. For example, a doctor could trick someone into betraying information by creating a false impression that the conversation would be held in confidence. However, any competent psychiatrist should be able to recognize mental illness in either hostages or terrorists—and note mental deterioration and perhaps even developing psychosis in them. Psychiatrists could advise about general physical well-being, and would know when more sophisticated medical advice is required. They would also be able to note signs of stress and strain in police officers at the scene, and advise periods of rest accordingly.

To Whom Are You Accountable?

The psychiatrist must answer this question *before* beginning work. There is no more destructive confusion at a moment of crisis than a confusion of accountability. I have already indicated that on matters of conscience doctors are accountable to themselves and to the wider ethics of the profession. However, in matters of decisions within an acceptable ethical framework, the psychiatrist, in my view, should be accountable to the senior police officer in charge of the operation.

How Do You Assess Your Effectiveness?

This is perhaps the hardest question posed by Cohen et al., and it is particularly important. If doctors are to be involved in this kind of work, empirical evidence must be developed to prove the value of their contributions. The profession's image and consequent public faith in doctors are at stake. With such high odds, risks must be precisely balanced with potential benefits. Therefore, the effectiveness of medical practitioners participating in this work *must* be evaluated. The police authorities themselves may resist such research. But the psychiatrists involved must persist. Such evaluation is essential.

CONCLUSION

Finally, I present four guidelines for doctors working with police in handling the problems of terrorism:

1. Doctors should stick strictly to their professional skills and, even under pressure, not claim knowledge they do not possess.
2. Doctors cannot relinquish their medical status. The techniques adopted by a doctor when working for a law enforcement agency must be compatible with internationally acceptable standards of medical and psychiatric practice. No practitioner should adopt lower ethical standards for terrorists or criminals than for others.
3. Doctors should remember that to collaborate with

an organization is tantamount to accepting the objectives and methods of that organization. If any organization flouts the principles of health ethics laid down by the World Health Organization, then doctors should refuse to work for or collaborate with such an organization.

4. Therapeutic relationships should be used exclusively for treatment purposes. If a doctor needs to talk for nontherapeutic purposes to an individual during a siege, then the nature of the interview should be clarified at the outset.

REFERENCES

1. Scott PD: The psychiatry of kidnapping and hostage taking. Proceedings of the Medical Association for the Prevention of War 3:47–61, 1978.
2. Clouser KD: Medical ethics: some uses, abuses, and limitations. *New England Journal of Medicine* 293:384–387, 1975.
3. Moore RA: Ethics in the practice of psychiatry: origins, functions, models, and enforcement. *American Journal of Psychiatry* 135:157–163, 1978.
4. Blomquist O: What is psychiatry and what is ethics? *Psychiatric Annals* 8:35–43, 1978.
5. Bowden P: Medical practice: defendants and prisoners? *Journal of Medical Ethics* 2:163–172, 1976.
6. Ochberg F, Gunn J: The psychiatrist and the policemen: ethical issues. *Psychiatric Annals* 10(5):30–45(190–201), May 1980.
7. World Psychiatric Association: Declaration of Hawaii. *British Medical Journal* 2:1204–1205, 1977.

8. Curran D: Psychiatry limited. Proceedings of the Royal Society of Medicine 45:105–108, 1952.
9. Lewis AJ: Health as a social concept. *British Journal of Sociology* 4:109–124, 1953.
10. Miller HG: Psychiatry: medicine or magic? *World Medicine* 5:44, 1969.
11. Shepherd M: A critical appraisal of contemporary psychiatry. *Comprehensive Psychiatry* 12:302–320, 1971.
12. Ochberg F et al.: Intervening in Community Crisis: An Introduction for Psychiatrists. Washington DC: American Psychiatric Association, 1977, p 42–43.
13. World Health Organization: Health aspects of avoidable maltreatment of prisoners and detainees. Presented to Fifth UN Congress on the Prevention of Crime and the Treatment of Offenders, New York, September 1–12, 1975.
14. Cohen R, Spraskin RP, Oglesby S, Claiborn WL: *Working with Police Agencies*. New York: Human Sciences Press, 1976.

3

Ethics in Hostage Encounters

BURR EICHELMAN, M.D., PH.D.
AND JOHN LION, M.D.

The Task Force on the Psychi-
atric Aspects of Terrorism and Its Victims has spent a sub-
stantial amount of time and energy examining the ethical
implications of psychiatric intervention in terrorist and
hostage-taking situations. This effort has moved through
several phases that culminated in the document in Appendix A. This chapter reflects elements of the process that
Task Force members underwent in generating this document. The process itself was, in retrospect, guided by underlying assumptions. These are that:

1. Ethics connotes an open-ended, reflective activity;
   a process rather than a static body of knowledge.
2. The ethical dilemmas of a given hostage situation
   can be better conceptualized when reflected in the
   light of overarching general ethical principles.
3. Ethical dilemmas are not necessarily rooted in conflict between right and wrong, but more frequently

in conflict between two competing ethical principles.

4. Case studies of hostage events, factual or fictitious, allow for individual reflection and peer dialogue that better prepare us for dealing with ethical dilemmas in emergent, rapidly moving hostage events.

5. Applying ethical principles to specific situations is an involved process. It requires reflection and dialogue as well as a weighing of competing ethical principles. Therefore, rules of conduct for psychiatrists in hostage situations must be general.

ETHICS AS A PROCESS

When an organization begins to examine its behavior and the behavior of its members, it risks having to draw up and enforce yet another code of conduct, a complex process at best. But legislating and enforcing codes isn't always the only (or best) way to deal with ethical issues. Professor John Ladd of Brown University, a member of the Committee on Scientific Freedom and Responsibility of the American Association for the Advancement of Science, expressed his committee's general position:

1. Ethics is an open-ended, reflective, and critical intellectual activity. It is essentially problematic and controversial, both as far as its principles are concerned and in its application. These principles are not the kind of thing that can be settled by fiat, by agreement, or by authority (such as by professional associations).

2. The attempt, such as by professional associations, to impose principles on others in the guise of ethics contradicts the notion of ethics itself, which presumes that persons are autonomous moral agents.

3. Attached disciplinary procedures and sanctions to the principles that one calls "ethical" automatically convert them into legal rules or quasilegal rules, conventions, or regulations.
4. The role of ethics is to evaluate, criticize, and sometimes even defend (or condemn) rules, regulations, and procedures, the social and political goals of organizations, and the institutionalized roles and activities of, for example, the professions.[1]

In this spirit, we present the material in this chapter.

GENERAL ETHICAL PRINCIPLES

We believe that a familiarity with general ethical principles will better prepare an individual to make sound ethical decisions in a hostage situation. These overarching ethical principles can be used as a basis for analyzing the moral dilemmas in various psychiatrist-hostage situations. Moreover, referring to these principles allows a case analysis to transcend the specific situation and guide ethical behavior in future situations.

Ethical principles have a long history within the traditions of philosophy. Therefore, understanding the historical development of ethical principles can be most useful. We encourage dialogue between clinicians and philosophers to better educate the clinician in the history of ethical principles.

Particularly useful principles in relation to the ethics of hostage situations include the philosophic constructs of respect for persons, justice as reflected by utilitarianism and distributive justice, fidelity to role, and the deontological aspects of truth and freedom—that is, the belief that truth and freedom are good in and of themselves and need not be ethically justified.

Respect for Persons

The principle of respect for persons was set forth initially by Kant.[2] Though it can be elaborated upon and developed along different lines, this principle states essentially that human beings merit respect because of their actuality of or potential for being rational—that is, self-affirming, self-determining, and rule-following. Respect at least involves taking into account the feelings, aspirations, and potentials of the individual. Some might suggest that offering respect includes attempting to maximize the opportunities for the individual to achieve his or her potential and goals. Offering respect precludes the possibility of treating the individual as an object, solely as a means to an end.

Harris expressed the corollaries of respect in the following way:

- Each and every person should be regarded as worthy of consideration, and should be so treated.
- No person should be regarded by another as a mere possession, or used as a mere instrument, or treated as a mere obstacle, to another's satisfaction.
- Persons are not and ought never to be treated in any undertaking as mere expendables.[3]

Distributive Justice

A philosophical definition of justice is equal treatment for all members of one and the same essential category. Distributive justice provides guidelines for the ethical distribution of finite resources or of such elements as risks and benefits.

The principles of distributive justice have evolved through time. In his utilitarian philosophy, John Stuart Mill argued for a distribution of wealth that would guarantee the greatest ratio of good over evil.[4] This moral calculus, though, sidestepped the question of what to do when a special few garnered all the good and left little for the larger group. Karl Marx attempted to define a just allocation of resources as "from each according to his ability, to each according to his need."[5] More recently, John Rawls, in *A Theory of Justice*, set forth the idea that a distribution is just if it favors the least advantaged members of a society.[6]

The ethical ideal expressed in distributive justice can be applied to the hostage situation. Translated into more concrete terms, the distribution of risks in a hostage situation can fall upon the hostage-takers, the police, the victims, or other participants such as psychiatrists. The benefits of participating in the risk-taking venture are considerably different for the psychiatrist and the hostages. Several ways of looking at the just method of allocating risks and benefits can influence decisions on what the moral expectations of participation are for the different parties involved.

Fidelity to Role

Psychiatrists can also base their behavior on the principle of fidelity to role. Throughout the centuries, society has afforded physicians many privileges not afforded others: the authority to handle and dispense drugs; the right, within reason, to invoke a mantle of confidentiality. In return, physicians are expected to respect patients and not abuse these special privileges for political, economic, sexual, or other ends.

Deontological Aspects

Lastly, the deontological perspective argues that certain behaviors are good in and of themselves. For example, one can argue that the pursuit of truth is good, as is the creation of music or art. Deontological perspectives can assert that the enhancement of freedom or the pursuit of truth are morally good behaviors.

The Task Force established the following ethical guidelines to help physicians act responsibly in circumstances where there is conflict between ethical ideals and the physician is called upon to act (these are detailed in full in Appendix A):

- In those circumstances where the psychiatrist is functioning in the role of a clinician, most specifically where he or she engages in a direct physician-patient relationship, the Task Force acknowledges that all elements of the American Medical Association's Principles of Medical Ethics with Annotations Especially Applicable to Psychiatry[7] should be upheld.
- When a psychiatrist intervenes outside of a patient-physician relationship or is called on to offer professional expertise outside the practice of psychiatry as a healing art and science, he or she must be guided by broader ethical principles.

CASE CONSIDERATIONS

The rest of this chapter describes how the above guidelines can be applied to specific situations. Readers are encouraged to discuss these cases with their peers and, in doing so, draw on their own experiences.

Case One

Scenario. One afternoon a university psychiatrist receives an emergency call from the state police. Apparently, one of his patients is holding a hostage at gunpoint aboard an airplane at a local airport. The police say the hijacker has asked to see this psychiatrist in particular. The police refuse to reveal the name of the hijacker, but insist that the psychiatrist appear at the airport and talk to the patient.

The psychiatrist is rushed to the airport, and he and a priest also requested by the hijacker are asked to approach the plane, unprotected against gunfire, the psychiatrist leading the way. Radio communication is established with the hijacker. As it happens, he is not the psychiatrist's patient, although the psychiatrist did see him once in consultation. At the request of the police, the psychiatrist assists in convincing the hijacker to leave the plane, whereupon he is immediately apprehended by the FBI and local police. Ultimately, the hijacker is incarcerated for twenty years. The city's mayor offers to present the psychiatrist with a commendation. The psychiatrist refuses, in part because he feels he was used by the law enforcement officers.

Reflections. At least two ethical principles in this case appear. First, the Kantian principle of respect for persons argues against treating an individual as an object, solely as a means to an end. Secondly, the principle of fidelity to role raises serious questions regarding the legitimacy of a physician being involved in a nonmedical encounter deceptively portrayed as a medical situation and where deception may be the strategic element.

In this situation, the psychiatrist perceived himself as having been manipulated by the law enforcement personnel. He felt that he had become an object, a pawn, used to solve the crisis. He was given incomplete information and the name of the hijacker was withheld. In fact, the psychiatrist was led to believe that the hijacker was one of his patients. Had this been true, the psychiatrist might well have had a continuing clinical relationship with the patient and therefore a bona fide clinical and ethical obligation to respond to his patient's crisis. In fact, however, there was no ongoing relationship, only a single, distant, consultation.

Second, the police placed the demands of the hijacker and the resolution of the crisis ahead of the clinician's safety. He was left exposed on the tarmac and vulnerable to gunfire from the hijacker. While police officers risk their lives as part of their role, that risk is foreign to the psychiatrist and not part of his or her established role. By assigning that risk to the psychiatrist, the police unfairly distributed the risks in this situation. The climate of the crisis placed considerable pressure on the psychiatrist to acquiesce. Not cooperating seemed untenable: The police had identified the hijacker as his patient; refusing to respond under such circumstances could have tarnished the psychiatrist's professional image.

This hostage episode illustrates the confusion inherent in deciding which role is appropriate, that of physician or that of citizen. Was there a physician-patient relationship in this hijacking? Can there ever be such a relationship operating in the crisis environment of a hostage event? Clearly, in this situation the physician did not acknowledge such a relationship.

Even if there had been a prior relationship, the rules governing that relationship are altered. The psychiatrist must ask to whom he or she owes allegiance. To the police, as representatives of society? To the hostages? To the hostage-taker, or his or her family and other patients?

By helping the police resolve a crisis, the psychiatrist

might inadvertently act against a patient-hijacker's best interests. In this case, the hijacker was coaxed into the open and then subdued by two law officers hidden at the side of the airplane. These officers had the option to subdue or shoot—an option totally beyond the clinician's influence.

The clinician's lack of control in the hostage event may even foster deception. The police may not only ask the clinician to knowingly cooperate in a deception, but also deceive the psychiatrist or override any assurances the psychiatrist has promised the hostage-taker. Recently, for example, a psychiatric resident assisted in negotiating a hostage release with the condition that the hostage-taker be taken to a psychiatric ward. But after the hostage-taker was captured, the police officer in charge overrode this assurance and the man was taken to jail. Not only did the resident feel deceived and used, but also feared the hostage-taker would retaliate when released.

Is there a body of clinical knowledge known to psychiatrists that justifies their involvement in hostage events? Very few American psychiatrists have had the negotiating experience commonplace in the FBI or a large city police department. Of course a clinician's relationship with a patient or his or her understanding of the psychopathology or psychodynamics of the hostage situation might well substantially offset the advantage of previous front-line negotiating experience.

These reflections place the caveats of John Gunn's chapter into a practical framework. Once the telephone rings or the police have come to escort one into the crisis event, reflection becomes exceedingly difficult. Asking the advice of peers is usually impossible. Further, the emotional current of the event seeks action rather than reflection, consultation, and delay. Unless clinicians have thought through what roles they could play during such an event, they become exceedingly vulnerable to the tides of the moment. They may make decisions they will later regret.

Case Two*

Scenario. You are a psychiatrist on the staff of a large urban hospital that includes facilities for the criminally insane. One morning, a man phones you who identifies himself as the captain of the Special Operations Division of the Metropolitan Police Department. He tells you that three patients from your hospital are holding a young mother and three small children hostage, in return for money, an armored car, and arrangements for a plane to Cuba. One of these patients had been in a program you supervise for the behavior modification of rapists. While you do not know the other two, you recognize them as men who have committed several murders, have been diagnosed as paranoid schizophrenics, and are considered extremely dangerous. The police captain wants you to tell him over the telephone everything you can that will help him secure the safety of the hostages and the surrender of the escaped patients. He wants you to come to the scene to be available to consult with the negotiators and, if possible, talk over the telephone with the patient you treated.

Do you immediately tell the police captain what you know about each patient? If so, do you offer generalities or specific details? Do you promise to call him back within a few minutes, after seeking approval from the hospital superintendent, or legal counsel, or both? Do you agree to join the police at the scene? Do you agree to talk to

*Provided by Frank Ochberg, M.D.

your patient when it becomes clear that he or she wants to use you as an intermediary?

Reflections. As a point of departure in discussing this scenario, Dr. Ochberg has provided one psychiatrist's response:

> I would begin with some generally helpful comments, assuming that in this extraordinary circumstance I was indeed talking to a police officer who is under considerable pressure. However, I would seek some excuse within the opening minute or two to break off and call him back for the sole purpose of establishing that his call is coming from police headquarters and that he is the person he represents himself to be. Within a public institution, I would seek approval from my next highest level of seniority to talk in depth to the police department about patient information. And I would certainly seek approval to attend the crime scene. I would not personally seek legal counsel, but would leave this to my institution's administration.
>
> At the scene I would do all in my power by imparting accurate clinical information: information about friends and family members who might influence the outcome positively or negatively, information about prior assault episodes and the circumstances that inhibited or exacerbated assaultive behavior. I would give all this information to the police attempting to control the scene.
>
> The fact that one patient was personally in my care and the other two were not would be immaterial to me once I confirmed that innocent lives were threatened and that the duly constituted public authority was attempting to save these lives. The patients had escaped from a hospital to which they were committed by the courts. The public, the profession, and the majority of patients themselves expect such cooperation between doctors and police officers in this type of circumstance. I see no ethical dilemma here for a psychiatrist.

Case Three †

Scenario. You are called at home by a lieutenant of your local police department who is acting as negotiator in an ongoing hostage incident. He informs you that Mr. A, whom you have seen regularly over several years for psychotherapy and medication treatment, has taken several hostages in the executive offices of the company from which he was just fired. He has mentioned seeing you but says that he does not want to talk to you now, and that he will solve the problem himself. He is threatening one hostage with a knife and claims to have planted explosives at several locations in the building. These explosives are set to go off if he does not deactivate them before his deadline, which is eight hours away. You remember that this patient discussed a fantasy of his with you, a plan he described as "something I'd do only if I were really desperate." While describing his fantasy, he named the places in the building where he thought people would never look for explosives. What, if anything, should you tell the negotiator, and do you need your patient's consent?

Reflections. Case 3 directly confronts the issue of the physician's role. Can the physician disengage from a situation that involves his or her patient? This situation suggests that the physician, by virtue of his or her continuing relationship with the patient, has a duty to "do no harm," or at least to attempt to minimize harm both for potential victim and patient. But to do no harm in this case conflicts with the issue of respecting confidentiality.

Both California law as illustrated by the *Tarasoff* de-

†Provided by David Soskis, M.D.

cision and the AMA Principles of Medical Ethics[7] appear to support breaking confidentiality and helping locate the explosives. The APA notes that the psychiatrist may "find it necessary in order to protect a patient or the community from imminent danger to reveal confidential information disclosed by the patient."[8]

Case Four‡

Scenario. You are consulting with a police department in the management of an ongoing hostage incident. It is clear from the hostage-taker's written demands and from what you have been able to piece together from conversations you have heard that he is actively psychotic. His brother tells you that the hostage-taker has been hospitalized five times—both for depression and for mania—and that he was doing well until he stopped taking his lithium one week ago. The hostage-taker does appear to be showing pressure of speech, flight of ideas, and grandiose delusions. The patient's brother asks "Couldn't you put some lithium in the food you're sending him?" Should you?

Reflections. Case 4 raises the two issues of fidelity to role and deception. There is no indication that the hostage-taker is prepared to enter into a therapeutic relationship with the physician nor has there been any legal authorization to deal with the individual as a patient and to treat him involuntarily. Thus, the physician is being asked to use his knowledge of psychopharmacology in a nonclinical situation to control the patient's behavior. This kind of intervention necessitates deception since the hostage-taker would not willingly accept medication. Even if one can

‡ Ibid.

disregard the pharmacology aspect—lithium would require a week or more to become effective and alternative
antipsychotic agents could cause dangerous side effects—
one must still deal squarely with the deception.

Many of the Task Force members were troubled by a
clinician's use of deception to resolve a hostage event.
These members seriously doubted, in this case, whether
the psychiatrist could truly be free of his or her clinical
mantle. And that this, in turn, would pose serious credibility issues for mental health workers within conventional
patient-therapist relationships. The short-term advantage
of successful deception might well undermine the traditional therapist-client relationship—and even tarnish the
reputation of clinicians as good-faith negotiators.

Case Five §

Scenario. You have been asked to help in a hostage incident in which the hostage-taker is holding his estranged
wife and two children at gunpoint. He has no prior psychiatric history and has said that he is willing to speak to
a psychiatrist and will not harm him. You have been
brought up to the doorway of the house in which the hostage-taker is located. You are standing about ten feet from
the door. The hostage-taker understands that he cannot
talk with you while he is armed. He has put the gun down
on a table near the door while he speaks to you. He is
having trouble hearing you and is beginning to edge out
of the door so that he can hear you better. He does not
know that police officers on either side of the door will
grab him as soon as he comes far enough out. You can see

§ Ibid.

both officers approaching the door. Should you warn the hostage-taker about the police?

Reflections. Case 5 illustrates a more passive deception. The psychiatrist is pressured to comply with the police in an effort to capture and subdue the hostage-taker. Again, this raises the issue of whether such compliance, in effect, tarnishes the clinician's mantle of trustworthiness. What if the police had to shoot the hostage-taker?

SUMMARY

This chapter proposes that attention to ethical issues for the psychiatrist in hostage situations requires a continuing process of review and reflection. The clinician can undertake such reflection with peers. Portions of this reflection should be done in advance of potential hostage situations by the use of case examples. Such case analysis is assisted by the examination of general overarching ethical principles and the observation that many ethically difficult situations involve tension between two or more ethical principles.

REFERENCES

1. Ladd J: Abstracts of a paper presented at the November workshop on professional ethics of the AAAS Committee on Scientific Freedom and Responsibility, 1979.
2. Kant I: *Groundwork of the Metaphysic of Morals.* Translated and analyzed by Paton HJ. New York: Harper & Row, 1964.
3. Harris EE: Respect for persons. In *Ethics and Society.* Ed-

ited by DeGeorge RT. Garden City, New Jersey: Anchor Doubleday, 1966, p 113.

4. Mill JS: *Utilitarianism*. New York: The Bobbs-Merrill Company, 1957.

5. Marx K: Capital. In *Capital, The Communist Manifesto and Other Writings of Karl Marx*. Edited by Eastman M. New York: Carlton House, 1920.

6. Rawls J: *A Theory of Justice*. Cambridge, Massachusetts: Harvard University Press, 1971.

7. The principles of medical ethics and annotations especially applicable to psychiatry. *American Journal of Psychiatry* 130:1058–1064, 1973.

8. Ibid., p 1063.

Part Two

The Victim

The Victim

Introduction

BURR EICHELMAN, M.D., PH.D.

The two chapters in this section deal with the victims—how they respond during captivity, and how they adjust afterward. Dr. Symonds has interviewed many victims of crime in his role as a consulting psychiatrist to the New York City Police Department. His clinical experience with victims vivifies his description of the psychology of the hostage event. Perhaps most important are his suggestions on how victims should be treated immediately following rescue and during the first stages of supportive counseling.

Dr. Ochberg discusses the victims of international terrorism such as those victimized by the Moluccan train hijacking. He describes in some detail the Stockholm Syndrome, a paradoxical behavioral pattern of attachment that can develop between hostage and captor. Rescue attempts can go awry because of this syndrome. Further, treating the syndrome, as Dr. Ochberg illustrates, is a major therapeutic issue.

4

Victimization and Rehabilitative Treatment

MARTIN SYMONDS, M.D.

The victim plays a pivotal part in any terrorist or hostage-taking situation. In many respects, he may be the most needy and appropriate focus of a psychiatrist's attention. Fortunately, political terror in the United States has not been as severe as in other countries. Consequently, we have fewer victims of political terror. But criminal terror here has its victims. I believe that the clinical experience of working with these victims will help us understand and assist *all* victims of terrorism and hostage-taking.

The chapter first describes the types of violence criminals use to terrorize victims and how victims respond—during and after captivity. Then the chapter examines the psychiatric treatment that has thus far proved most effective for these victims.

Three categories of crimes involve sudden, unexpected violence. Each differs in the degree of contact between criminal and victim. The first is that in which there is no victim contact with the criminal at all. Burglary is an example; violence, if it occurs, is directed toward property, not persons. The second is composed of crimes with minimal contact between criminal and victim. Street assault and robbery, popularly known as mugging, fit into this class of crime. The third category includes crimes in which there is prolonged criminal-victim contact. Examples of this type are rape, kidnapping, and hostage-taking.

My work with victims of all three categories has yielded some interesting findings. Regardless of type of crime, victims' responses to the incident follow an almost immutable pattern. This pattern is characterized by four distinct phases. The sequence of these phases is always the same, though the duration and intensity of each can vary depending upon the nature of the victim's contact—if any—with the criminal.

The first two phases are acute. Phase one is denial, characterized by shock and disbelief. Phase two occurs when the denial is overwhelmed by the sense of reality, at which point the victim's behavior is characterized by responses such as frozen fright, clinging, and compulsive talking.

After a period of time that varies from victim to victim, the individual enters phase three. In this phase the victim's behavior is marked by traumatic depression and self-recrimination. The depression is characterized by circular bouts of apathy and resignation, irritability, suppressed rage, insomnia, stark reactions, and continual replay of the traumatic events through fantasy and nightmare. Typically, the self-recrimination is expressed in the victims' feeling that they were "stupid"—both for leaving themselves open to victimization and for the way they behaved subsequently. Of course, in evaluating their actions, victims use a standard of "normal" behavior; they do not allow for the situation's traumatizing effect. It is in this phase that earlier victim-specific personality patterns and experiences exert an influence on the person's behavior. Individuals who had been excessively dependent on others are prone to develop more constricting, depressive behavior. Their fears increase, phobic responses develop, and quite often such victims form hostile-dependent relations with family and friends. Individuals who had been regressive or predominantly detached from others tend to become more removed and shorter tempered. In effect, these persons have said, "The world is a jungle, and to hell with being Mr. Goodguy."

As victims begin to adapt and integrate the traumatic experience into their behavior, they enter phase four, a period of resolution and integration. In this phase individuals develop defense mechanisms to minimize or prevent future victimization. In this last phase, victims often experience a profound change in values and attitudes—toward both people and possessions—that can be directly traced to the effect of the incident. For example, people whose homes have been burglarized reduce their personal involvement in property. Jewelry, watches, TV sets become mere replaceable objects. They reason that, by divesting their selves from their property, never again will they be so painfully vulnerable.

Some individuals are unable or unwilling to accept their victimization and integrate it into their future behavior. It may be impossible for them to reach phase four. Such an individual experiences his victimization as a personal affront to his pride. His feelings are compounded by his perception that society is indifferent to his plight. He embraces his feelings of rage and injustice, and constantly seeks reparations, even revenge, for his victimization. In this sense he will remain psychologically disabled.

In the crime of burglary, the victim does not come in contact with the criminal at all. So the criminal does not witness the victim's response. I will focus primarily on victims who pass through the acute phases while in the criminal's company—for example, as in the crimes of kidnapping and hostage-taking.

A criminal's purpose in using a dramatic threat of violence is to induce terror in his victims, so as to render them helpless and totally submissive. Terror, an affective state defined as extreme fright, may take many forms. To fully understand a victim's responses to criminally induced terror, I explored people's general reactions to terror. This past year I asked several acquaintances and colleagues whether they had ever experienced terror and, if so, when and how they dealt with it.

All the nearly 100 people I asked said they had felt terrified at some time in their lives. But most recounted experiences related to unpredictable or frightening *events* rather than people. One person had awakened to a room filled with smoke. Another's plane had caught fire midway across the Atlantic. This man, recalling the episode, said he had just sat still in his seat, reviewed his life, and hoped death would be sudden. A third person had developed a cramp while swimming and thought she would never get back to shore.

There is a popular misconception that individuals respond to sudden, overwhelming danger with mindless screaming or running, or even catatonia. This misconception is abetted by the media: In today's paper I read about a woman who, when her hair caught fire, had jumped three floors to her death. Neither the behavior of victims nor first-person accounts of catastrophes wholly support this notion.

Situations of sudden, overwhelming danger can be classified as one of two kinds: those in which there exists the *potential* for escape, and those in which no escape is possible. In situations of the first type where the potential for escape is extremely slim, individuals *may* exhibit terror in the form of mindless running or acts of desperation. For instance, a victim may jump five stories from a burning building, throw himself out of a moving car in which he is held captive, or flail about at a bee while driving down the highway at sixty miles an hour. Another example is when a child who feels abandoned runs and cries in desperation. Paradoxically, when his parent reappears, the child will probably cling to this very person who "abandoned" him. I will return later to this theme of clinging to the very source of the terror.

For a hostage, though, no escape is possible: the captor has blocked all possible exits. Under these conditions, the victim responds to this sudden, overwhelming threat to his life with a paralysis of affect. The terrorized victim is frozen, even while his cognitive and motor functions remain operational. Affect is split from the motor and cognitive functions.

Of course, undercover agents and others in dangerous work occasionally suspend affect. But this process, to the contrary, makes the individual hyperalert. These persons are on a high; they see everything. Terrorized individuals, on the other hand, undergo a *paralysis* of affect, accompanied by a narrow constriction of their cognitive and motor functions.

The behavioral manifestations of this paralysis may or may not be dramatic. The victim may seem calm, even friendly. In fact, the majority of terrorized individuals don such a cooperative, friendly "mask." The masquerade serves to conceal the paralyzed affect.

I first became aware of this form of frozen fright when I interviewed an eight-year-old incest victim some years ago. During the interview, she was bright, vivacious, voluble, and very cooperative. At the end of the interview I said, "You can go now." She took a deep breath, sighed heavily, and said, "I never thought I'd get out of here alive." Obviously, she had perceived the interview as a no-exit situation. In hindsight, I had noted no evidence that the child was frightened during the interview. But in the twenty years since, I have seen the same sort of frozen fright in many victims.

On the other hand, the manifestations of frozen fright may be quite dramatic. Some victims—particularly the young or immature—may cry, tremble, or cling. Despite these histrionics, their affect is still frozen, and will thaw only when the danger subsides.

Let me illustrate with the story of some hostages held during a recent robbery. During the robbery, a youngster, one of several hostages, began to cry uncontrollably. Despite the efforts of the robbers and the other victims to quiet her, she persisted. Finally, one of the robbers shot her to death. Dog owners will recognize another example of the behavior I am describing. When there is thunder my dog trembles, cries, and clings. There is nothing I can do to stop him, not soothing, not yelling, nothing. The only thing that works is the cessation of the thunder. Then he becomes his happy self again. This is frozen fright.

A hostage undergoes a sequence of experiences. First the victim comprehends his entrapment: There is no escape; all hope of freedom is in the hands of the terrorist, who completely controls the environment. Second, the victim slips into a state of frozen fright. All hopes for survival are focused on the terrorist. The terrorist encourages this reaction by thwarting any attempts by the victim to reduce his own powerlessness. Third, the victim begins to feel completely isolated. In fact, where there is prolonged contact with the criminal, each victim invariably talks as if he were the only one involved—whether or not he is just one of several victims. In his mind, the victim develops an exclusive one-to-one relationship between himself and the criminals. For example, when a group of people is robbed, the victims don't talk about how *they* were robbed; each talks about how *he* was robbed, how *he* was scared.

Karen Horney terms this feeling of isolation and helplessness *basic anxiety*. An individual beset by basic anxiety responds with primitive adaptive behavior. Adaptive responses learned in maturity evaporate, to be replaced with infantile survival mechanisms. I call this response in victims *traumatic psychological infantilism*. It compels an individual to cling to the very person who is endangering his life, just as the terrified child I described earlier clung to the parent who "abandoned" him. At this point, victims become placid and compliant. If the atmosphere of terror persists, the psychologically traumatized victim perceives that the terrorist, who wields the power of life and death, has chosen to let the victim live. Then a very profound behavioral and attitudinal reaction occurs within the victim: Now he sees the terrorist as a "good guy." This phenomenon is called *pathological transference*.

I have witnessed this phenomenon many times—in men, women, and children—under conditions where the victim perceives an extreme threat to life. For example, an undercover detective making a narcotics purchase was held captive for three-and-one-half hours while the drug dealers debated whether to kill him. Eventually, the leader decided not to kill him. Finally, the officer's backup team discovered his whereabouts and freed him.

I interviewed this man two months later, in the presence of his superior officers. He kept assuring me that the gang leader was a "good guy" even as his fellow officers displayed an arrest record an inch thick. The detective said, "No, he's a good guy. He didn't kill me," and was reluctant to testify against the gang leader. Yet this detective was a man working in law enforcement.

Another detective, while off duty, accidentally stumbled on a robbery. The robbers discovered he was a detective when they frisked him and found his badge and gun. The three pointed their weapons menacingly and kept saying, "Let's waste him." They even put a bag over his head, forced him to his knees, and nudged his head with their gun muzzles. But the detective kept hearing one of them say, "Aw, leave him alone, let's not kill him." After a while the robbers left. Some time later the "benevolent" robber was captured in another incident. The detective who had been held captive was on the scene. He said to the robber, "I owe you. I'll take care of you. If you need me I'll be there for you because you were there when I needed you." Again, we had difficulty convincing this detective that the robber was one of the bad guys; he saw him as a good guy.

Pathological transference often occurs between children and parents who abuse them. For ten years, I consulted to a residential home for youngsters who had been so brutalized. In that time, rarely did one complain of how his parents had treated him. Obviously, pathological transference had occurred. The parents had repeatedly threatened the lives of their children, but had stopped short of killing them. The children felt their parents had "let them live."

Whenever the criminal or terrorist actually shoots at the victim, pathological transference will not occur. Gunfire destroys any potential for pathological transference. Pathological transference can occur only when the criminal deliberates and does not shoot.

Pathological transference consistently occurs in hostages held by criminal terrorists. Hostage victims are essentially instruments used by the captor to exert leverage on a third party, whether the hostage's family, the police, or the government. The captor's threats of extreme violence to the victim are meant mainly to coerce the third party. Thus the captor gives the victim the illusion that the latter is safe as long as the third party gives in to his demands. This manipulation lays the groundwork for a very intense pathological transference, especially when the hostage has already been psychologically traumatized by terror. These two components, traumatic psychological infantilism and pathological transference, are probably the crucial elements in the Stockholm syndrome.

Several implications can be drawn from our understanding of what the victim undergoes and how he psychologically reacts to his experiences. I would like to suggest some groundwork for psychological first aid to victims while they are still in the hostage situation as well as for treating them immediately after their release. I would also like to submit some principles for helping hostages whose reactions to victimization are delayed, but persist for some time after their release.

Though I have no hard data to support this recommendation, I believe that while the person is being held hostage it is best not to disturb the pathological transference with the captor. Any attempt to do so may reactivate the terror and cause the victim to lose all hope. In the terrorized, such hopelessness generally results in an act of despair or panic.

However, one *could* also argue for attempting to reduce the hostage's feeling of isolation. Perhaps a link could be established between the hostage and the outside world. For example, it might be possible to relay an innocuous message to the hostage through the terrorist—something like one of the victim's coworkers has told the boss that the victim won't be able to work the next day. Sending such a message may be taking a considered risk, since often the victim behaves like an ostrich, in order to make himself less noticeable to the captor. Singling him out by sending such a message may, therefore, traumatize the hostage or even precipitate a reaction by the terrorist. So I hold to my first tenet of not interfering with the pathological transference.

Another tactic has been used by a Dutch psychiatrist. He tries to reinforce the transference by only partially meeting the physical demands of the terrorists—that is, providing only some of the food and other supplies requested in order to induce shortages or insufficiently satisfy the hostage-taker's needs. The psychiatrist's purpose was to anneal the bond between the terrorist and the victims through mutual suffering. This was an attempt to cause the terrorists to perceive the victims as part of their group, which might then decrease the risk to the victims.

My second tenet is that, given the unpredictable effects of pathological infantilism and pathological transference on the victim, it is unwise to make any plans that depend on the victim's participation. To a terrorized person, an open door is not an open door; he perceives danger everywhere.

Immediately after his release, skillful psychological management of the victim is crucial. The therapist must reverse the very factors that fostered his psychological infantilism: the hostile environment, the victim's feeling of isolation and helplessness.

First and foremost, the victim must be assured that he is no longer surrounded by a hostile environment. At this point, the victim needs a nurturing environment in which he no longer feels isolated. Subsequently, it is crucial to restore a feeling of power to the victim. Consider that the criminal has taken the victim's pride, and has completely controlled his body and possessions. Both therapists and police must allow time to restore a feeling of power in the victim. Debriefing the victim immediately after the release just takes more from him, at a time when he has little left to give. When I teach police officers how to deal with a recently released victim, I often encourage them to defer to the victim for his permission: "Is this a good time to talk to you?" "Is this place all right?" "Are you comfortable?" This restores the victim's power to choose, thus reducing his sense of helplessness.

Any effective plan of treatment must allow for a hostile reaction by the victim. Not every victim is tremendously grateful that he has been released. Often he is just angry. The very fact that there was bargaining for his life can anger the victim. That a victim's release is being negotiated for indicates that a third party has set a price on how much he is worth. The victim himself, on the other hand, would give anything and everything for his release. So victims always have a built-in hostility toward the people who negotiate their release.

About fifteen years ago I viewed a very interesting film about a normal four-year-old child who was taken to a hospital for a tonsillectomy. The film illustrates how this child, who was left crying in the hospital, developed a residue of hostility. After his parents left, the child would not respond to any kind of nurturing. Ultimately, he quieted down, underwent the operation, and three days later was taken home by his parents. As the child was walking down the hospital stairs with his parents, he kicked his mother. I think we have to allow for kicking by victims. Even though others may help immeasurably in their release, there is still a tremendous amount of latent hostility in victims. It is important to allow for the expression of that anger.

Finally, treatment must allow for and work with the fact that victims frequently have fantasies of revenge, many of which are impossible to execute. How can victims get even with someone who has humiliated and brutalized them—often in a most degrading way?

Sometimes justice does seem to side with the criminal. In one case in which I was involved, a woman had been shot in the chest, and her daughter had been shot in the mouth, cutting her tongue in half. Luckily we sutured successfully, but the bullet remains in the daughter's neck because removing it might compromise the facial nerve. The criminal, who lives in their neighborhood, is out free. He walks past their house and thumbs his nose at them. The child and the mother hide behind the couch and watch TV. They live in fear that he may come back and shoot them. We all know that bullets travel in a straight line. Nonetheless, terror has so distorted their perception, that they feel a bullet can make a complete circle and hit them where they hide.

What is "getting even," and how can this need of a victim be met? One thing I have learned from people who have lived in the ghettos and people who have been in concentration camps is that by surviving they are getting even. The very fact that the victim survives ultimately thwarts the criminal's efforts. Every time a victim is not afraid, he reduces the criminal's power to hurt him; every time he is afraid, he enhances that power. The victims of concentration camps couldn't kill Hitler, but the fact that he didn't kill them means that they won.

We in the helping professions can assist victims of terrorists to cope successfully with meeting their needs to get even. We can try to develop within these victims the feeling that they have succeeded in getting even by the act of surviving the terrorist situation.

5

Hostage Victims*

FRANK OCHBERG, M.D.

In the wake of the dramatic, dangerous, and tragic events in Iran, world attention focused on the phenomenon of terrorism and the ordeal of hostages. The response of victims to being taken hostage in terrorist situations has been the subject of dozens of recent interdisciplinary, international conferences, scattered case studies, and the literature pertaining to related but different circumstances: prisoners of war, concentration camp survivors, victims of natural disaster, and victims of crime, particularly rape and spouse abuse. This much seems generally accepted:

- Many hostage survivors do quite well. The crisis provides an opportunity for survivors to reassess their values and critical relationships with others. Many feel, after the experience, that they have "a new lease

---

*This chapter is adapted from Ochberg, FM: Victims of terrorism. *Journal of Clinical Psychiatry* 41:73–75, 1980.

on life." None would want to repeat the experience, of course, but many contend that life has, in some way, become more precious.

- Another group of victims is remarkably untouched. Dr. Wilhem Van Dijk examined the Dutch survivors of the Moluccan train hijacking in northern Holland in 1977. He found that the rural folk, who maintained a stoic outlook and were nonpsychologically minded, remained remarkably untouched by the incident.
- Some victims are clearly affected and suffer psychological symptoms but, fearing stigma, avoid seeking psychiatric help.
- Some victims suffer and do seek help. Between one-third and one-half of the ex-hostages I have known fall into the last two groups. Many of victims' families are also in these categories. Family members suffer as surrogates and as anguished, frustrated witnesses, yet are unprotected and unsupported by the physiological responses and social network available to the hostage.

The victimization † hostages experience can be either uncomplicated or pathological. Following the crisis, the hostages may abuse drugs, become depressed, or develop other psychological problems. They may remain under the influence of the Stockholm syndrome, a bond that forms between hostage and captor during the event. These clinical consequences of victimization have implications both for the immediate management of a hostage event and for

----

† Although many people may feel like victims from time to time, here the term *victimization* is used to describe a narrowly defined set of events where one individual is physically assaulted by another.

the subsequent treatment of hostages seeking mental health counseling.

Uncomplicated victimization is one class of posttraumatic reaction. The victim feels powerless, and responds with resignation or rage; but this effect is transitory and does not seriously impair his self-esteem.

Pathological victimization, on the other hand, either impairs the victim's self-esteem or disrupts his life for an extended period of time. The concept of pathological victimization is similar to Lindemann's concept of uncomplicated pathological grief. The effect of uncomplicated victimization, though it may be quite strong, is transitory. The effect of pathological victimization is extreme in intensity or duration and disrupts the individual's ego functions.

Victims of assault may suffer pathological grief as well as pathological victimization. Moreover, they may become preoccupied with imagery of death; in the hostage situation, the veil of denial that mercifully shields our conscious mind from images of our own death may be abruptly pulled back. This preoccupation with death imagery can continue after the victim's release; it can overwhelm an individual by inducing gross anxiety attacks, nightmares, phobias, obsessions, or other debilitating defense mechanisms.

Hostage victims report many psychological sequelae, including nightmares, startle reactions, and phobias. For instance, one-third of the Dutch ex-hostages developed train phobias. Some would not ride a train at all, some would ride only with a trusted friend or relative. Others would ride only to Assen, where the hijacking occurred, and then would have to transfer to a bus to Groningen. Few hostages report nightmares during captivity, but nightmares are common for a week or two after a hostage is released. Children may have protracted problems with nightmares, and may re-enact the trauma in play. Drugs, alcohol, and tobacco are common ways of coping with this crescendo of anxiety.

A hostage may not suffer depression until after the post-release clamor subsides. Hostages emerging from notorious events are celebrities for some time and also may have forged strong emotional relationships with other hostages—and even with captors. As their celebrity recedes and as the relationships are relinquished, depression may occur. Other problems have also been noted, including paranoid reactions, obsessions, and various idiosyncratic adjustment difficulties.

The Stockholm syndrome is one psychological sequela of sufficient interest to merit more detailed comment. The term originated in Sweden in 1974 during an incident in which Olsson, a bank robber, held Kristin, a bank employee, hostage for several days, and the two emerged very much in love. Furthermore, Kristin publicly berated the Swedish prime minister during and after the incident for his failure to understand Olsson's point of view.

This syndrome develops frequently in hostage events. It has affected hostages and captors of all ages, both sexes, and many nationalities. The syndrome seems to develop during the opening chaotic moments and increases in intensity during ensuing calm periods. It may last several years. The positive feeling that originates in the hostage is not identification with the aggressor, but rather a pathological transference based on terror, gratitude, and infantile dependence. However, hostages can consciously prevent the syndrome. Businessmen on the train seized by the Moluccans cautioned younger hostages against forming attachments to their captors. These businessmen wanted to avoid any support for the group, which had struck several times in their small community. Similarly, the Moluccans wished to avoid attachment to their victims, and remained aloof.

I believe that in the Stockholm syndrome three conditions may be present, singly or in combination. They are: positive feelings by the hostage for the hostage-taker; positive feelings reciprocated by the hostage-taker for the hostage; and negative feelings on the part of the hostage for the authorities responsible for rescue. The best explanation I can offer for the first condition, the positive feelings of captive for captor, is that captivity makes the individual so infantile and so frightened that he recovers a certain primitive, unconscious, positive feeling. This feeling can be traced to the way the infant feels trust, pleasure, and something like gratitude for the parent who removes the aversive conditions of infancy: the helplessness, the hunger, the wetness, and the isolation. This positive infantile feeling is the precursor of love, affection, and trust.

Adults who experience this feeling in captivity obviously do not understand it as infantile affection. They translate the feeling into emotions that are appropriate for their age and sex, and then act accordingly. A senior Italian magistrate, held captive by young terrorists, told me that he regarded them as his own children. A restaurateur held in the London Spaghetti House siege described his relationship with his captors in avuncular terms. Kristin clearly expressed her feelings in heterosexual love.

The captors are more likely to reciprocate when they are terrorized and when the hostages are potential exit visas for safe passage to another country. Of course, in a situation like the 1980 takeover of the U.S. embassy in Iran, this condition does not exist. The victims are more like prisoners than hostages; the captors do not need to fear for their lives.

There are four important implications for siege managers stemming from the Stockholm syndrome. First, the hostage cannot be trusted, cannot be given advance warning of an attack, and cannot be depended on for reliable information about conditions inside the siege room. Second, the hostage may be useless as a witness for the prosecution after the event. Third, the hostage, with a world audience, may broadcast a message of great comfort to terrorists everywhere. Fourth, the Stockholm syndrome locks captive and captor in a bond that promotes the survival of each. For this reason, it is the policy of American police training programs to promote the development of the Stockholm syndrome.

As awareness of the sequelae of hostage events becomes greater, clinicians may encounter greater demand for services for victims and their families. This demand may be further augmented by the attention paid to hostage victims by the press. Psychiatrists, by providing a sanctuary for exploring unconscious material, might well help ex-hostages extricate themselves from the aftermath of their captivity with minimal loss to their self-esteem and social functioning.

Part Three

Training Law Enforcement Personnel

Training Law Enforcement Personnel

Introduction

DAVID SOSKIS, M.D.

A decade has passed since international terrorism, ushered in by the triple skyjacking of three airliners by Palestinian terrorists in September 1970, first emerged as a major phenomenon in the history of the 20th century. Probably one of the most accurate analyses of this phenomenon was provided by one of the terrorists himself, as he attempted to explain his actions: "It was a severe entry into their minds; nevertheless it was an entry. They had to ask the question: Who are these? Why are they doing that?"* We have succumbed to many other "severe entries" since that time, and have had the opportunity to ask and try to answer many difficult questions. When Palestinian terrorists struck again during the Munich Olympic Games in 1972, the whole world, including the United States, became worried spectators.

Over the last ten years we have learned to live with

---

*Interview on ABC television program "Hostage," January 30, 1978.

terrorism and hostage incidents, and the next three chapters will focus on the evolution of a characteristically North American approach to our share of this problem—the discipline of hostage negotiation and how it is taught to the law enforcement professionals who practice it. Before beginning this subject, however, it may be useful to examine some of the broader perspectives that have emerged from this traumatic decade.

The attack on the Israeli athletes during the Munich Olympics was a clear message to the world that the old rules no longer applied. For many Americans this could not have been communicated in a more dramatic way than through a flagrant disregard of the code of sportsmanship and the "friendly" competition of the Olympic Games. The location of the games served to remind some observers of the bitter lesson of the Holocaust: that human nature is fully capable of the worst, not just by deranged individuals, but by organized groups who believe sincerely that what they do is justified.

It would be a mistake, however, to lose sight of a basic and seemingly contradictory presupposition that underlies all hostage incidents—that individual human life does indeed have value. It is this presupposition that makes hostage-taking such an intensely personal form of conflict in the midst of an increasingly technological society. It is shared commitment to the value of human life that unites the hostage-taker, hostages, and authorities in the tense triadic relationship that makes hostage negotiation possible.

There are, to be sure, many situations where this presupposition does not operate. Where the aim is only to kill, we have assassination. Where the victim does not value his own life, we have suicide. Where he values it less than some deeply held belief, we have martyrdom. Where the victim is a soldier who accepts the risks of combat we have a prisoner of war—but not a hostage. Finally, when the action occurs in a society that places no value on individual life, as in many totalitarian states, there is simply no game—nothing to negotiate.

Thus it is within the context of a strong value placed on individual human life that the discipline of hostage negotiation has evolved in North America. Like many of our other native disciplines it is intensely pragmatic, having been forged in the fires of necessity on the front lines of actual hostage incidents rather than in the remote coolness of some ivory tower. It is no small irony that it took terrorism, with its image of sophisticated weaponry and manipulation of the electronic communications media, to focus attention on one of the least acknowledged but most potent of law enforcement tools—the development and control of human relationships. Detectives skilled at interrogation or in cultivating informers have always valued and used this tool, but it has never been as visible as the service revolver or the flak-jacket.

The effective hostage negotiator uses the development of human relationships among all the parties involved in a hostage incident to bring it to a peaceful conclusion. An adequate theoretical framework for this process has yet to be developed and, as with many scientific advances that have benefitted mankind, its development will follow rather than precede the development of potent helping tools. One potentially useful theoretical model for hostage events, though, is provided by game theory. Most hostage-takers enter an incident viewing it as a win-or-lose proposition, what game theory terms a zero-sum game. In zero-sum games (such as chess) what one player wins is, by definition, lost by another. This model applies most clearly to crimes such as burglary: I have taken (won) your television set and you have lost it.

As crimes shift away from property and move into the area of interpersonal violence, however, it becomes harder to identify what it is that one side wins and the other loses. In murder, one player loses everything and it is difficult, though not impossible, to describe what the other player gains. Certainly, it is virtually impossible in murder or terrorist situations to specify what can be given back to redress the wrong. There is no property that can be returned to the victim after the trial, and the whole idea of turning to the terrorist for redress is seen to be irrelevant.

There is, however, another type of game described by game theory. That is the non-zero-sum, or cooperative, game, where one player's winning is not linked rigidly by the rules to another's losing. An example would be the bidding or buying game in which the prize will be time-shared. Here there may be several winners and no loser, everyone may lose, or many other variations. The process of a successful hostage negotiation may be defined as the transformation of a zero-sum game ("If we don't get all we demand, then we've lost and you've won") into a cooperative game ("In this resolution, we've both won and no one has lost"). It remains to be seen whether this model can lead to useful planning and prediction as well as illuminating what has already occurred.

The three chapters that follow are far from theoretical. Those by Frank Bolz and Conrad Hassel provide the reader with an opportunity to share in the developing thought of two of the pioneers in the practice and teaching of hostage negotiation in the United States. The discipline of hostage negotiation, in fact, had its beginning in the work of Frank

Bolz and Harvey Schlossberg in the New York City Police Department. Captain Bolz outlines this history and gives us a glimpse into the interaction of planning and chance that have determined how and by whom negotiation would be practiced. He reviews the other options for resolving hostage situations—assault, sharpshooters, and chemical agents—from the perspective of a police professional familiar with the realistic costs and risks. His chapter concludes with a unique view of the psychological and interpersonal stresses that are involved in the option he himself pioneered—hostage negotiation. An understanding of these stresses should contribute to planning for the second generation of hostage-negotiator training programs.

The second chapter in this section is by Special Agent Conrad Hassel of the Federal Bureau of Investigation. Mr. Hassel, whose professional background is in law and criminology, shares his experiences in the development of a training program for hostage negotiators at the Special Operations and Research Unit of the FBI Academy. This program has been attended by senior law enforcement and military officers from all regions of the United States. His discussion covers issues of student selection, evaluation, and integration of what the student negotiator has learned into the administrative and human realities of his own department.

In the United States, a high percentage of hostage incidents involve hostage-takers who clearly have mental disorders, and Mr. Hassel explores the evolving relationship between law enforcement and behavioral science professionals that has been crucial in the development of techniques for negotiating with such hostage-takers. In the course of his exploration, he probes the differences in background, philosophy, and habit that have complicated this evolving professional collaboration. It was in the course offered by Mr. Hassel's unit that Dr. Frank Ochberg, Dr. Sharon Wainright, and I learned as students and gained experience as teachers. A lawyer deeply committed to the protection of civil rights, Mr. Hassel extends his discussion to some of the constitutional issues raised by our efforts to contain and deal with terrorism, including questions of the legal definition of terrorist crimes, the influence of diplomatic and foreign policy issues, and abuses of and proposed restrictions on freedom of the press.

My own chapter, which concludes the section, focuses on the relationship Mr. Hassel describes between law enforcement and behavioral science professionals in developing techniques for the optimal resolution of hostage incidents. I discuss the results of an empirical study that explored the reactions of and decisions made by representative samples of both groups in response to a hypothetical terrorist hostage-taking incident. The results provide the raw material for refining our working alliance, and may give grounds for some realistic optimism as well as provide some surprises for readers holding some common preconceptions.

My chapter concludes with a review of my experiences in teaching the psychiatric aspects of hostage negotiation to law enforcement officers in Mr. Hassel's course and in other settings. Problems both sides have in establishing a functional consulting relationship are reviewed, and suggestions are offered for resolving them. I outline my approach to teaching, which places special emphasis on psychosomatic disorders, severe depressions, and paranoid schizophrenia—an approach that may provide useful guidelines to other mental health professionals involved in the field, but that by no means exhausts the range of effective approaches to the task. My own presentations are largely didactic, and are supplemented in the FBI Academy course by intensive role-playing under the supervision of David Swink of St. Elizabeth's Hospital in Washington, D.C. This kind of supervised practice is crucial for integrating classroom learning with the negotiator's personal style of communication and the stresses inherent in real hostage incidents.

Taken together, the chapters in this section attempt to provide professionals in law enforcement and mental health, and those responsible for broader issues of policy and planning, with a functional perspective on how the discipline of hostage negotiation came to be, and on the resources and problems of those who collaborate in its practice. In the face of the new barbarism of international terrorism, this collaborative practice is something the United States can justifiably be proud of: the saving of lives by law enforcement officers not by means of deadly force, but through the establishment of trusting human relationships in the face of the most severe human conflict and distress.

6

The Hostage Situation:
Law Enforcement Options*

FRANK BOLZ, JR.

The field of hostage negotiation was created out of necessity and shaped by practitioners rather than theoreticians. My own background is probably fairly typical of those who forged the principles of hostage negotiation out of experience "on the street." I grew up in a working class family in Brooklyn and spent thirteen years at night school to get my baccalaureate degree. This kind of a background has made me, and my colleagues, incurably practical.

The real impetus for development of this field came in response to the hostage-taking at the Munich Olympics in 1972. I was fortunate in having had the opportunity to visit Munich one year before the incident, and to meet Manfried Schreiber, the Munich Police Commissioner. After the incident I was able to learn a good deal about

*The material presented by the author represents his own opinions and perceptions and does not necessarily reflect the policies of the New York City Police Department.

what had happened through the contacts I had established. Following the incident many people were very critical of the way it was handled and extremely worried that similar incidents would occur in the United States. Actually, from the standpoint of law enforcement, many of the aspects of that incident were handled well, though unsuccessfully. Above all, we learned the importance of having complete intelligence and excellent communication among all the people involved in an operation. Commissioner Schreiber was generous in sharing with us what he had learned and we moved forward from that point.

From these beginnings, the New York City Police Department put together a set of guidelines to deal with hostage confrontations. These guidelines are structured for our own system but can be used with slight modifications in any department, whether it be a 6-member police department or a 24,000-member force such as ours. The guidelines are formulated so that they are merely that: guidelines. They are not step-by-step instructions or rules on how something has to be done.

My focus in this chapter will be first to present the basic options open to the law enforcement professionals who are in charge of managing hostage incidents. I will not attempt to explore the psychological factors that bring a hostage-taker to a particular position. Rather, I will deal with the incident as it unfolds, as it presents us with material with which to work. Second, I will discuss, using specific incidents, some of the psychological and interpersonal stresses on the negotiator.

THE ASSAULT OPTION

From a law enforcement perspective, the first course of action for resolving a hostage incident is a direct assault.

In some ways, this is the option with which the conventional police officer is most comfortable. In New York City, our tactical team is called the "Emergency Service Unit." It basically is a rescue operation. Officers might rescue someone pinned inside an automobile, or someone lodged under a subway car, or someone jumping from a bridge. Their basic goal is to preserve life and their attempts are not always successful. This same group serves as our tactical-assault squad. The way this combination of roles evolved was natural because rescue work of all kinds—be it rescuing a hostage or someone attempting suicide—requires specialized equipment as well as specialized vehicles to transport it. All 260 members of the tactical team are experts in both roles. The dual nature of the job has been very beneficial to team members because it minimizes the negative psychological effects of working on a tactical unit and having to be prepared to use deadly physical force.

No matter how well an operation is planned, or how well people are prepared, there is often some loss of life. When a person takes a human life, inevitably there is some psychological scarring; in some people it can be more traumatic than in others. I saw this most clearly when I was in charge of the old "stake-out unit" of the New York City Police Department. This was a unit of forty specially trained men whose assignment was to sit in the back of a store that was expected to be held up. Our men would wait until the holdup was completed and the complainant was out of the line of fire, and then would step out from behind a partition and announce themselves: "Police, don't move." If the perpetrators turned in the direction of the police and pointed a loaded weapon at them, our men would fire.

An example of the most severe form the negative psychological effects could take occurred after I had left the unit, which remained in operation for another two-and-a-half years. One of my colleagues explained to me that an officer who had already killed three people in the line of duty was in another shoot-out in which a man was fatally shot. The commanders at the scene recognized the potential trauma for this officer. The officer said "I want to call my wife," and the supervisor responded "Go ahead, sure, call your wife." At this point the officer picked up the phone and said "Hi Hon, I'll be a little late for supper. Yeah, I bagged another one. What do you want me to bring home? Milk, yeah. What else? Yeah, toilet paper. I'll be a couple hours late. See you soon. Goodbye."

For me, listening to that story was a very traumatic experience. It made me feel that we had done this man and men like him a serious disservice when we set up that kind of operation. In the course of three years of operation, this unit killed approximately fifty people, creating something of a problem for the officers involved. Should someone give people a reward or a promotion for killing? Yet this was work that had to be done.

Recently there has been a serious epidemic of bank robberies in New York City. I was asked to arrange for the training of a new unit to handle this problem. This time, because of the knowledge I had gained from my previous experiences, we set up the unit a little differently. We included careful psychological examinations, such as the Minnesota Multiphasic Personality Inventory (MMPI), to help screen out officers who are depressed or might otherwise seek out life-threatening situations. In addition, we gave each of the officers selected for the unit a day-and-a-half of special sensitivity training. The purpose of this training was to communicate our recognition of what might happen to them if they had to use deadly physical force, to let them know what to expect, and to tell them that such an occurrence would surely be something out of the ordinary for them. We also tried to increase the officers' receptiveness to getting psychological help if they found events becoming overwhelming. We found that the term "stress" and the concept of "stress prevention" are much more acceptable to our officers than the mention of psychiatric therapy.

In general, however, the officers in the Emergency Service Unit have considerable built-in psychological reserve that helps them withstand the pressures they often must undergo. If they do have to take life, their day-to-day involvement in rescue work helps them recognize that they have taken every other step possible before choosing this irreversible option.

A major factor in the self-confidence of the officers in this unit has to do with their actual preparedness for even the assault option. What is needed to go through with this option? Of course, one needs background intelligence about the situation and the ability to communicate this intelligence to others. For example, in a hostage situation it is crucial to know the number of hostages, the number of perpetrators, what kind of weapons are involved, the floor plan of the building, and many other relevant details. In several instances hostage-takers have disguised themselves as hostages or merely changed clothes with the hostages, as the hostage-takers did in the Attica riot. In addition, criminals who are part of an operation such as a robbery attempt sometimes secrete themselves in the building ahead of time to back-up their cohorts.

THE SHARPSHOOTER OPTION

The second course of action open to law enforcement or military personnel is to use a sharpshooter. Here again, background intelligence and the ability to communicate it are crucial. On a technical level, all the officers in our unit are highly qualified with a sniper rifle: Each is able to place ten out of ten rounds in a target the size of a silver dollar at seventy-five yards.

This kind of training and preparation, however, addresses only the technical aspects of the situation. A tragic incident that took place in California exemplifies the problems that can complicate even the best technical plans, and the limitations of irreversible options.

A young man about twenty-five years old, with long blond hair, was holding three people hostage on the second floor of a building. He had a rifle. The following description of him was disseminated by observers: male, white, long blond hair, with a long weapon. About three hours into the incident the hostage-taker, becoming nervous, wanted to find out the locations of the surrounding police. He unloaded the rifle, gave it to one of the hostages (while retaining a small handgun), and pushed him over to the window. Unfortunately, that hostage also was male, white, young, and with long blond hair. When he came to the window with the rifle, one of the sharpshooters across the street recognized the description, took careful aim, and killed the hostage. The hostage-taker surrendered shortly thereafter.

This kind of tragedy emphasizes the differences between actual hostage incidents and the common media portrayals, especially in popular television shows. The typical tactical unit in such a show is composed of handsome young men, all in their mid-twenties, who are always running. They never seem to walk anywhere. Our own police officers average 39.8 years of age; our emergency service people, our tactical team, average 44.5 years. If you tell one of our officers to run here or run there he'll probably say "Wait a minute. When the Policemen's Benevolent Association gets us running money we'll run; in the meantime we'll walk." This is not an inappropriate response. These officers bring with their years a certain amount of maturity and judgment, the most valuable commodities that one can bring to a hostage crisis.

A good example of the role this kind of judgment can play in hostage incidents is seen in a "push-out," a situation in which the perpetrator exits from a building holding a gun, often cocked, against the hostage. On television shows, snipers make dramatic, long-range shots in situations like this. In reality, the risk involved seldom justifies this option. Even if a perpetrator is shot in the head, the final reflex reaction may be just enough to squeeze off the two-and-one-half pounds of pressure that will fire a cocked weapon. Instead of saving the life of the hostage, the police officer may be a catalyst in his death. With this in mind, when someone asks what we in the New York City Police Department do if confronted with a perpetrator who is going to do a push-out, we say "Let him go." When we are asked "How can you do that?" we bring up the issues of judgment and perspective mentioned above. Right now the New York City Courts Division has approximately 250,000 felony warrants outstanding. If one more person gets away it will not change this number significantly. The death of one innocent hostage, however, would be a terrible consequence.

There is a further reason for letting the push-out go

that has to do with the basic psychology of the hostage situation. When a person takes a hostage, it is because the hostage is important to the hostage-taker. The hostage gets him attention, and gives him protection. It is commonly believed that "Once he gets away, he'll kill her." In reality, most people killed in hostage situations die in exchanges of gunfire.

This does not apply to the kidnap situation in which the victim is being held secretly. Here there is no confrontation between the perpetrator and the police, and by murdering the kidnapped victim the kidnapper may be doing away with the only person who could identify him. In fact, we would advise a kidnap victim to say to the kidnapper: "Listen, I don't want to look at you. Not that I am disrespectful, but this way I will not be able to identify you. I'll never be able to know what you look like and therefore you won't have to worry about me." The worst thing that you could possibly say to a kidnapper would be "I'll never forget your face." It's likely, under those circumstances, that he'll help you forget it—permanently.

NONLETHAL FORCE—CHEMICAL AGENTS

The third course of action open to police officers in a hostage situation is to use nonlethal chemical agents such as tear gas. As with the other options this course of action takes background intelligence and the ability to communicate that intelligence accurately to all people involved. Here, however, another element is introduced: This intervention can affect all the hostages, the hostage-taker, or just one particular hostage whom he may be holding as a shield. Suppose one of the hostages has emphysema. Suppose there is a child who has very small lungs. Suppose the building itself contains very volatile fumes, is highly flammable, or has some other special condition.

From a tactical point of view, the police officer is faced with a choice between "hot gas" and "cold gas." Cold gas can be used in a volatile atmosphere. It is relatively safe, but does not disperse quickly. Eventually it will cloud up the room and take effect, but this may take some time. If one decides to use the hot gas, which is dispersed through actual burning, many other risks are involved, such as fire. More problems may be created than solved.

An area of special concern in using chemical agents is the ventilating system in the building or area where one is working. A ventilating system can sometimes be used to carry gas dispersed in one room to the room where the hostage-taker has sequestered himself and his victims. In the process, the hostages may be injured, panic, or both. Uninvolved occupants of the building, if they use the same ventilating system, could likewise be affected. In New York City we have had a chance to witness most of the problems that can arise. It is a frightening experience to throw tear gas into a building and then to watch it flowing out of the window and into a subway ventilation shaft. The subway driver is blinded by the tears and stops the train. People start to get off, not sure what is affecting them, and in the darkness of the tunnel run the risk of stumbling on the electrified third rail.

Ideally, chemical agents are used to avoid deadly physical force. Unfortunately, more gas is required to control people who are drunk, highly agitated, or in some other aroused emotional state than they can really tolerate physically.

The ramifications of using any chemical agent must be

thought out in advance. Sometimes even the best intentions can go astray.

NEGOTIATION

This brings us to the fourth course of action open to the law enforcement professional confronted with a hostage situation: negotiation. In the New York City Police Department this is the option with which we are most concerned and the one we have developed most fully. Our goal through this option is to contain the hostage-taker in the smallest area possible and to negotiate. We want to talk to him, let him ventilate, let him "get it out." We are willing to take the time to find out who he is and what he wants. We also want to give him an opportunity to let the world know about himself. Perhaps the reason for his actions is to obtain a stage; by allowing him to use the incident as the stage we may satisfy his need and thus avoid a tragedy.

It has often been said that letting someone ventilate in public will make it "the thing to do," that reinforcing the behavior will tend in itself to bring about more and more hostage incidents. Critics feel we should go in with an iron fist, crush any resistance, and bring the crisis to an end. Kill people if you must, they say, but show that we will not tolerate such criminal activity. Certainly there are some countries in the world that follow that kind of hard line; people who are at war or that consider themselves at war. In some countries, such as Israel, the government is *very* firm when it comes to terrorism. The authorities feel justified in using whatever force is necessary to bring an international or military incident to a conclusion. However, in their civil operations (which are similar to those in our own cities) they use the same techniques and tactics as the New York City Police Department.

Even if we grant some need to turn to prompt military assault in wartime or warlike situations, it does not seem as if assault has eliminated or significantly reduced the incidence of terrorism. Our own approach is to try to minimize hostage-taking incidents by treating those who engage in them as people who have psychological problems. We emphasize this perspective by making sure that hostage-takers, in addition to being criminally charged, undergo a psychiatric examination. Everybody wants to be a hero, but nobody wants to be a "psycho." We try to remove the heroic sense of these actions and place the perpetrator in the context of a person with a mental disorder.

THE CHOICE OF NEGOTIATION

Obviously, the first three courses of action described above are violent. They are all alternatives that tactical commanders must have ready and available in the event that containment and negotiation fail. But if such a course is started, the participants are committed to it. Once engaged in violence one can't stop and say "Finis. We want to stop what we are doing now and talk with you." On the other hand, if the first strategy is that of containment and negotiation, one can escalate later into one of the more violent forms of intervention.

One of the gains from first using containment and negotiation is time. Time is incredibly valuable in hostage situations. Time permits the assembling of equipment and manpower and, most importantly, the assembling and communication of intelligence. There is time to think, to plan, and to try to arrive at a rational and practical course of action.

In addition to helping the law enforcement officers on the scene act more rationally and effectively, the passage of time leads to the development of ongoing relationships between the hostage-takers and the hostages. The best known of these is the "Stockholm syndrome," which involves the development of positive feelings in the hostages toward the hostage-takers, often accompanied by negative feelings toward the police. Such relationships are useful to some extent and may make the course of the incident more predictable; they tend to keep all participants alive and contribute to a successful resolution of the crisis.

We believe that the strategy of containment and negotiation has proved itself in the years since the Munich Olympics. Although negotiation has been less successful in resolving incidents of political terrorism that have occurred around the world, it seems to be the preferred technique for dealing with the typical North American hostage-taking, which more often is committed by a person with a mental disorder or by a thwarted felon. In evaluating this technique it is important to compare it with the other realistic alternatives I have discussed. Despite what we see on television or in the movies, each of these more active (or violent) methods, in addition to being irreversible, has its own characteristic risks and drawbacks. Containment and negotiation as a response need not be granted special favors for "humanitarian" reasons in practice, it has proved the most successful way of resolving hostage incidents.

PSYCHOLOGICAL AND INTERPERSONAL STRESSES ON THE NEGOTIATOR

One thing that has emerged from our experience with the process of negotiation is a sense for the problems of the negotiators themselves. I have experienced some of these myself. One such incident occurred during the course of a supermarket robbery that evolved into an incident involving forty-two hostages. The robbery had not gone well and the three perpetrators—one armed with a sawed-off rifle, another with a handgun, the third with a machete—got greedy when they couldn't open the safe. Not satisfied with the money in the cash tills, they began to rob individual customers in the store. That, for them, was the crucial mistake.

Someone saw the robbery and reported it to the police. Because the criminals had taken so much time inside the store, the officers arrived while the robbery was still in progress. The responding officers contained the robbers, and the Emergency Service Unit was called. The Hostage Negotiating Team, which I head, was also notified and we soon reported to the scene. Everything seemed to be going pretty well: We had progressed from our initial telephone contact with the perpetrators to a face-to-face contact. While I was walking back and forth in the "frozen zone" of the inner perimeter, I saw an off-duty policeman with his brother. Both had been allowed through because the officer was wearing a shield. We knew each other and had worked together. He said "Frank, do me a favor. My niece is in that store. This is her father. If you get a chance to trade any hostages, get her out first." This was a tremendously heavy burden for me. Before that

I hadn't known anybody in the store; the hostages were all equally important to me. If any of them were lost, I knew I would cry at the end of that incident, no matter which hostage it was. Now the situation was changed because I knew the identity of one hostage.

I have since tried to spare other negotiators this sort of experience. I have tried to teach commanders that if there is an off-duty policeman or someone in the area who has relatives inside, he *must* be kept away from the negotiators.

The emotional balance of the primary negotiator can be protected by structuring the negotiations. We try to set up a "negotiating module" with a primary negotiator, a secondary negotiator, and a coach. We also have other negotiators who feed intelligence into that module. The coach and the secondary negotiator act as insulation between the outside world and the primary negotiator, who is interacting directly with the hostage-taker.

There is a second feature of the incident just described that was stressful for me personally and that emphasizes some of the problems of managing hostage-taking situations. The perpetrators had used a young woman as a shield, holding a gun to her head much of the time as they walked back and forth. Occasionally the perpetrator would point the gun at my partner and at me; occasionally he would put it to the woman's or another hostage's head. This went on for about two hours. This particular woman was a pretty twenty-year-old who reminded me of my own daughter of about the same age.

Three days after the incident was over I received a four-page letter from the woman's family. First they thanked us and blessed us profusely for our efforts. Then they spent three pages berating us for not taking the time to care for the families of the hostages during the incident. To be sure, the families were kept nearby in a church. But the attention given them was nowhere near proportionate to the suffering they were going through.

It is really impossible for negotiators to be in charge of this part of the operation too. Dealing one-on-one with a hostage-taker demands all their attention. Certainly the families of the victims are also victims themselves. Their needs must be attended to by the overall commander of the situation.

The families of hostages can provide some valuable assistance to the negotiators in the protective "module." The families will have a great deal of information about the personal and medical histories of the people inside. From them negotiators will be able to learn, for example, if a particular hostage might try to do something like disarm the perpetrator.

One of the most difficult decisions facing a commander is what to do if the captor kills one of the hostages. A killing tends to move a police commander toward one of the more violent, irreversible solutions, since it says that negotiation, at least as it has gone to that point, is not enough to keep the hostage-taker from killing. Unless one has decided to take a rigid "If A happens, we will do B" approach, it is important to find out what actually happened. Was the hostage-taker provoked or frightened by one of the hostages? Or did he execute a hostage who was cooperating and acting submissively? Families and friends of hostages, again, can provide clues to whether hostages they know might have provoked the hostage-taker. An unprovoked killing clearly suggests a greater danger to surviving hostages.

Considerations such as these clarify the fundamental

differences in the style of thinking behind a military operation and a law enforcement operation. There is no such thing as an "acceptable" casualty rate to a police department or other local law enforcement agency. Many military commanders are accustomed to thinking in terms like, "In this operation we expect 10 percent of our people to be killed and 15 percent to be wounded." In civilian law enforcement the only acceptable casualty rate is zero. In general, the public echoes this kind of expectation and communicates clearly its disappointment and outrage when hostages are killed.

Another decision making conflict that is stressful to the negotiator and to the commander is the issue of keeping promises made to hostage-takers over the course of an incident. This is not an easy problem in terms of the legal point of view (because such agreements are made under duress), the moral point of view, and the effect on the negotiator's ability to function in future incidents within a given community. Some claim that hostage-takers seldom know what has been promised in previous incidents, or whether such promises were kept by the officials who made them.

In New York, certainly as large a community as one could imagine, we have had some direct experience with the issue of making and keeping promises. In one particular incident a man was holding his wife and child hostage. A week before, he had been working in a prison where he met a hostage-taker with whom we had negotiated earlier. When we approached this new perpetrator and told him we were hostage negotiators and wanted to help him, he said "Oh yeah; you are those guys with the baseball hats and blue jackets. I heard about you in prison." He was familiar with the fact that we had allowed the earlier hostage-taker to spend some time with his wife and to have some wine before he gave up. Information about this earlier incident had gotten into the prison system and people were talking about it. The new hostage-taker now believed we would uphold everything we had promised him during our negotiations. He finally surrendered when we promised to take him for a ride through Prospect Park to see some trees before he went to jail. We took him into custody, put him in a car, and took him into the park; then we took him to jail. We did keep those relatively insignificant (to us) promises. Thus the relationship between keeping promises, credibility, and the conduct of a particular incident has to be judged individually on a cost-benefit basis.

Another area of stress for the hostage negotiator, which is not apparent to outside observers, is his need to maintain a sense of personal and professional pride in the negotiation process. Although the role of hostage negotiator carries some glamour and often leads to publicity, it also conveys a sense of vulnerability and openness to scrutiny that the average law enforcement professional does not have in his day-to-day work. If a negotiation goes poorly the responsible officer will suffer guilt and shame. There is little that can be done to counteract these feelings, although the support of friends and superiors—who will stick by him and prevent feelings of personal responsibility from becoming unrealistic—is important.

The role of support from "the top" in situations like this usually has been underestimated. Officers who are called names like "fascist pig" in confrontations with criminals or political demonstrators tend to respond in terms of threatened pride. A commander who says to his officers, "Listen, if you keep quiet and take it, I will respect you," provides a great deal of additional strength to a beleaguered officer. This perspective on the situation must be initiated and reinforced frequently by the officer's superiors. If the negotiator's pride can be preserved he is likely to function better in negotiations—and be that much better prepared for future incidents.

In the New York City Police Department the presence of Dr. Harvey Schlossberg—as both a senior law enforcement officer and a trained psychologist—was extremely helpful in recognizing the varied effects of stress on negotiators. Many of us had been unaware of the connection between what we were experiencing and what we felt. Typical symptoms are sleeplessness for hours after a hostage incident, the "shakes," nausea, and irritability. These symptoms can be particularly acute when incidents end late at night or early in the morning. Some of our negotiators have had problems in their marital relationships and all of them take the tensions of their experiences home with them.

We found that if an incident ended at three or four in the afternoon we would all retire to a local bistro, have something to eat, a couple of drinks, or sometimes just a Coke. It wasn't the alcohol, but rather the interaction of the group that helped all of us ventilate the anxiety of the incident. This is an important way to increase the efficiency and effectiveness of officers in these difficult assignments; I extend overtime pay to cover these informal "debriefings."

Many people at the command level are skeptical about the value of these debriefings but then many are still skeptical about the whole concept of hostage negotiation. This skepticism is best answered with results, which we have. This is a new area; we must be open to recognizing its unique stresses and to formulating innovative coping techniques.

7

Preparing Law Enforcement Personnel for Terrorist Incidents *

CONRAD HASSEL, M.S., J.D.

For some time now, the Special Operations and Research Unit I head at the FBI Academy in Quantico, Virginia, has been conducting training sessions on the principles of hostage negotiation for law enforcement officers from all parts of the United States. Although the Federal Bureau of Investigation has developed and pioneered many new programs, it is important to acknowledge that the discipline of hostage negotiation had its origins in the New York City Police Department through the efforts of Dr. Harvey Schlossberg, Captain Frank Bolz, and their colleagues. We learned a great deal from their experiences and adopted many of their methods.

We began by applying these methods to the training of our own agents in all of our field offices. However, it

*The material presented by the author represents his own opinions and perceptions, and does not necessarily reflect the policies of the Federal Bureau of Investigation.

became increasingly obvious that local police needed support in this area. So we decided to try to provide some of that support. We set up an intensive two-week training program. Class size is restricted to fifteen police officers—drawn from various communities throughout the United States. Admittedly, at this rate, it will take some time to train a sizable number of senior police officers. But we feel our program will make a stronger impact by concentrating on quality rather than quantity. Moreover, it is often difficult, with a larger group, to transmit the knowledge, attitudes, and skills that are crucial to making a successful hostage negotiator. Some of the educational experiences that we use, such as videotaped role-playing, are inherently individual methods and therefore very time consuming.

From an academic point of view, our effort certainly has been successful. With the help of several psychiatric consultants who regularly lecture to our people, and with the feedback we get from our agents and former trainees, we have been able to stay abreast of developments in the field and have obtained and maintained academic accreditation from the University of Virginia. In this chapter I would like to focus on some of the lessons we have learned from these experiences, especially those that reflect on the broad issues of the professional identity of the law enforcement officer and the possible responses by democratic countries to the phenomenon of terrorism and hostage situations.

Despite the fact that police officers represent one of the largest groups of helping professionals, their precise role in our society has never been fully defined. Many people seem to get their ideas of what police officers are from watching television shows like "S.W.A.T." Others see police officers as anything but helpful. The facts strongly contradict both these stereotypes. Several studies have shown that only about 20 percent of police officers' time is spent in activities directly related to catching criminals and that 60 to 80 percent of their time is spent in other kinds of public service.

While the public generally sees the police officer as probably the most visible agent of the "establishment," few people stop to think that police officers are the only helping professionals who still regularly make house calls. Only those who have experienced an emergency necessitating police assistance appreciate this particular function.

In our society, in fact, the police officer is the person most frequently called on to intervene in a crisis. In the larger, more sophisticated police departments, the concept of a police officer as expert in crisis intervention is understood and accepted. However, perhaps 80 percent or more of police in the United States are in very small police departments of fewer than 100 officers.

In these smaller police departments, officers find it harder to accept themselves in this role as a professional in crisis intervention, especially when it comes to intervening in family situations. These officers often consider such intervention "social work," not what they went into police work for, not an appropriate use of their skills and training. They are cops. Interestingly enough, such intervention in family crises is responsible for a very sizable number of police deaths, usually the number two or three cause in most surveys. Obviously, with this many deaths crisis intervention is truly dangerous work. So it *should* be seen as appropriate work for police, who are trained to be both technically and psychologically prepared for just these kinds of dangers.

How did these negative attitudes come about and why do they persist? Perhaps one reason can be traced to the background of most police officers and many FBI agents. We often come from lower-middle-class upwardly mobile families. My father, for instance, worked on the New York docks, and never finished high school. But he always said to me, "Education is very important; get an education." He surrounded me with good books and good music and always wanted to look at my report card. This is a typical police background: very conservative and upwardly mobile.

This may help explain why police react so negatively to rapid—what they often perceive as too rapid—social change. These emphatically negative reactions were especially marked in the 1960s, when young people in America were flouting the conservative social ideals many police held dear. Police found this situation difficult to face, and there were many accusations by behavioral scientists and others that police were brutal. In my opinion this was not an accurate characterization. They were reacting as their fathers would have to a son caught smoking pot in the corner of a flophouse or something similar. These police officers went in, grabbed the youngsters, and "talked to them by hand for a while." Certainly that is not what they should have done. But often they were just treating these young people as they would their own children, and as they themselves had been treated. It was not, for them, an unconcerned and purely hostile response. It is important to remember that police officers were no better prepared for the phenomena of the '60s than the rest of America.

This negative attitude can degenerate into what I call the "Blue Bastion" syndrome. Police who are victims of this syndrome sit around and complain to each other: "Ain't it a bitch, the world is falling apart and we're the only defenders of what is decent." Even more dangerous, police feeling this way will talk only to other police, thus blocking any opportunities to really learn about current social conditions. Fortunately this complete isolation has dissipated. The ending of the Vietnam War contributed to this, in part, through the consequent moderating of social protest. In addition, the gradually increasing professionalization of police work has brought us into closer working contact with professionals from other disciplines.

In essence, there has been a redefinition of what is and what is not police work. The whole field of hostage negotiation is a good example; it is now clearly considered a part—a prestigious part—of the law enforcement function. Both hostage negotiation and crisis intervention then, are part of this "new" definition of police work. In fact, in some ways these new fields relate to each other and contribute to each other's refinement. What, one might ask, does negotiating with a husband and wife have to do with negotiating with a hostage-taker? The answer is that they can be very similar. In a domestic dispute one or both of the partners is often armed, and these domestic disputes frequently lead directly to a hostage situation.

The field of hostage negotiation, on the basis of need, has brought us into contact with professionals in psychiatry and psychology. Our own statistics from the FBI reveal that close to half of American hostage-takers suffer from a significant mental disorder. In light of this knowledge, one does not have to bend the facts or reach for esoteric interpretations to see the clear relationship between police work and the behavioral sciences. It is most encouraging that a number of professionals in the behavioral sciences have begun to devote serious attention to these areas and to work in close collaboration with law enforcement agencies.

There are more specific psychological barriers that sometimes stand in the way of a police officer's responding appropriately to a terrorist incident or hostage situation. One of the most troublesome of these is the strong urge to *do* something, anything, but to take some kind of action even if it is wrong. It is very difficult for a police officer, by temperament and by training, to do nothing. Inaction is also a difficult posture for a military person, and these are the two groups that are most likely to be in charge of managing terrorist and hostage incidents.

Unfortunately, many times in a hostage situation this is exactly what you want to do: nothing. Doing nothing does not mean letting time slip idly by, but instead focusing on establishing communications, gathering intelligence, and just allowing for some emotional equilibrium to settle on the scene. Only with adequate knowledge and preparation can the appropriate action be decided on. Unfortunately, police officers and all of us to some degree feel personally threatened if we do not storm in there and kick down the door. In a way, such action says to the hostage-taker, "You can't do this to us, you can't, we won't allow it." It is important to free the police officer and the military man from this mental block so that they can do what is best in each situation—even if this involves remaining physically inactive for a long period of time.

For many hostage-takers in the United States, this kind of calm inactivity is especially crucial. In fact, that there has been an increase in hostage-taking in the United States is in a way a tribute to the increased efficiency of our police departments. We are now able to respond in two or three minutes to an armed robbery. It used to take fifteen minutes. Because of this shorter response time, more armed robbers are trapped in the liquor store or bank before they can escape. Thus the man who starts out as an armed robber becomes a hostage-taker. He has no specific political cause to espouse, but wants something rather less abstract: to get out. So he takes a hostage. In all probability this particular type of hostage-taker is not mentally ill. Yet it is important to remember that people under severe stress do not always act rationally. If we pressure him, if we are pressured ourselves either internally or externally toward precipitous action, we may drive a usually rational person toward irrationality.

All of us at some time or another have behaved irrationally under pressure. No doubt you can all remember such an instance when you were studying for an examination or working on your income tax. You feel tremendous pressure and someone, perhaps one of your children, comes in and bothers you about something. You break your pencil, scream at your own child, maybe even slap him, and yell "Can't you see that I am busy!" And the kid runs out. Then you start thinking: "Great gobs of guilt, what have I done?" You put down the broken pencil stub, find your child, pick him up, and say "I'm sorry." You say to yourself: "What's more important, my income tax or my children?" Nevertheless, your initial reaction was not a rational one. For those few moments, your view of life was kind of skewed. Yet this is a very human incident. Something similar has occurred to all of us. With this perspective it is much easier to understand how irrational action is distinctly possible in the high-stress hostage situation.

This kind of stress, of course, affects the negotiator as

well as the hostage-taker. One of the areas of deficiency in many training programs for hostage negotiators is in differentiating between how well various students handle these stresses. In the FBI, we train our own negotiators and we are able to hand pick the people we want to train. What's more, we have a good idea of their backgrounds beforehand. This helps us assess their educational resources, their work experience, and their personality—so that we can match the person to the job with a fair degree of accuracy. The selection process is much more difficult in a training program for people from other agencies. We try to give organizations who send us people to train a rough idea of the kind of person we want, what qualifications make for a good hostage negotiator, but different organizations interpret our criteria differently. For example, sometimes organizations see a ticket to our training program or to other specialized schools as a way to reward exemplary performance. So they send the chief of their S.W.A.T. team.

We could respond to these selection problems by making our academic examinations extremely difficult. But this would not get to the real problem. Of course, it helps if a trainee has the requisite knowledge. But a person's personality must also be suited for this work to allow appropriate knowledge to lead to appropriate attitudes and skills. Perhaps an officer who didn't pass the written examination would still make a good negotiator. We have acknowledged that our current selection and rating system is far from perfect and that basically what we can certify at this point is that the officer has completed our course.

In addition, even if a hostage negotiator is ideally suited to this kind of work and is well trained, he will have trouble functioning if his superiors do not really believe in this kind of approach. For some senior police officers and chiefs, negotiation as an activity is very threatening. As we speak to negotiators from around the country we find that two of the major stressors on their jobs are the attitudes of those higher up toward negotiation and the explicit or implicit pressures that contradict the approaches we have taught. Often the explicit or implicit message to the negotiator is: "I want you to resolve this situation immediately because we have a traffic jam downtown and you've got all the cops tied up. Let's get it resolved fast. I want you back here."

Unfortunately, this kind of thinking still pervades some police departments in the United States. It is impossible to approach such problems by telling our student negotiators, "This is the right way and there is no other" because in their particular situation this may *not* be the right way. Some things will work in one department and not another. In our own training sessions we try to cope with these potential conflicts by saying "This is how it has been done here, this is how it has been done there, and these are some of the strong and weak points of each approach." We long ago gave up saying "This is the FBI way to do it, the right way." Local variations are one of the main reasons why a "cookbook" approach to hostage negotiations has never been realistic.

As we turn from the specific issues of hostage negotiation to the broader area of terrorism, several perspectives emerge. Above all, it is important to remember that terrorism in the United States is not as serious in terms of a threat to our social system or economy as in other nations. This must be kept in mind when we weigh the risks and benefits of programs aimed at combating terrorism. That is not to say that terrorism has not had some marked successes. It has been dramatically successful in spawning an academic cottage industry. Researchers of every description are always trying to get funds from one federal agency or another to do something about terrorism. Terrorism has also been very successful in terms of publicity; in fact, its record in this area is spectacular. Whoever heard of Black September before Munich? Whoever heard of the Symbionese Liberation Army before Patty Hearst was kidnapped? When the TWA flight was kidnapped many people hadn't the slightest idea of who the Croatians were; one man had them confused with crustaceans and thought they were seafood. But today's news is still tomorrow's fish wrappings and it is important not to overestimate the value of the instant notoriety that terrorism brings.

A more realistic danger of terrorism and extremism (from both ends of the political spectrum) in the United States is the provocation of government over-reaction. Sophisticated revolutionaries know how unlikely it is that they will overthrow a relatively stable government on their own. They put more hope in provoking "antiterrorist" measures that will alienate large segments of the population from their government.

We have to be extremely careful in this country of this over-reaction. If there is any real, fundamental difference between "us" and "them" in this society, whoever they may be, it is the first ten amendments to the Constitution of the United States, the Bill of Rights. We will never be as efficient as the Gestapo, nor should we try to be. Mussolini was the only person who almost wiped out the Mafia, and even he did not quite succeed. In fact, often the only thing that stops people in power in our society from kicking down doors to defend the Constitution is the Constitution itself—in the form of the Bill of Rights. If we want to preserve these basic rights, we may have to accept some terrorism as the price. We must not lose liberty in the effort to defend it.

There is no specific mention of terrorism as a crime in Title 18 of the U.S. code, the criminal code of our country. Murder is a crime, kidnapping is a crime, extortion is a crime, and robbery is a crime. The safest way, for our society as a whole, to handle acts of terrorism is not to accept the criminals' definition of these acts as political "expropriations" or as "self defense." A bank robbery should be seen as a bank robbery and the people who commit it should be put in jail with other bank robbers after a fair trial. A murderer should be treated as a murderer; the righteous indignation of the terrorist certainly does not help his victim.

These perspectives become complicated when international acts of terrorism occur. In such situations the State Department is inevitably involved; and one of the major determinants of what is done can often be the aims and priorities of a foreign government. In a domestic situation there is much more that we can do and it is much easier for us to act on our own values. In addition, we really do have things to negotiate: We can give food, we can give money, we can give various other creature comforts, we can even give freedom if we have to; we have a lot of room to bargain and a lot of control over the outcome compared with an international situation.

One of the areas where we have little control, whether the terrorist incident be national or international, is in the press. The Hanafi case in Washington, D.C. was a good example of our lack of control and of the press's need to act on its own terms. The decision had to be made in that incident whether to "pull the plug" and not allow the subject to talk to anyone but the negotiators, or to allow him to speak freely. Khalis, the leader of the hostage-takers in this incident, had experienced the murder of several members of his family. Because of what was perceived as his profound need to ventilate his rage and frustration, he was allowed to talk. In that situation the press certainly made some errors. For instance, Khalis had a television and was able to watch T.V. shots of snipers on the roofs and people slipping in and out of the back of the building. It was difficult to balance the clearly positive value of Khalis' ventilating his long pent-up frustrations against the occasional provocations by irresponsible journalists and the fact that he could see as much as he did.

Whatever our theoretical position on freedom of the press, the fact is that in the United States there is no way we can control the press, nor should we be allowed to do so. This position is not always popular with police officers, but I believe that it is a sound one. We in law enforcement are never going to be friends with the press and we have with them what is in many ways a fundamentally adversary relationship. That adversary relationship should exist because members of the press may find out something that needs to be found out. Modern law enforcement professionals have to be able to tolerate these sometimes friendly, sometimes adversary relationships with other professional groups. If we grow as a profession we will deserve the respect that we want; and if our other professional colleagues, whether they be journalists, psychiatrists, or politicians, keep an open mind on what we have to do and how we must do it, we will get the respect we deserve.

8

Law Enforcement and Psychiatry: Forging the Working Alliance

DAVID SOSKIS, M.D.

It is the irresistible pressure of traumatic events and not any hidden element in their own personal agendas that has brought together law enforcement personnel and psychiatrists during terrorist and hostage incidents. Professionals in both groups may wish that terrorism would go away and leave them to the more routine and more easily managed aspects of their challenging work lives, but this is not to be the case in the immediate future. In the face of this reality, sobered (and one hopes educated) by their previous encounters, law enforcement officers and psychiatric personnel are working together again. There is some real evidence that both groups have learned from some of the mistakes made in their past collaborations—as in community crisis-resolution, for example. In fact, several cordial working alliances have already been formed.

This chapter, by reporting the results of an empirical study, will explore some of the possible foundations for such alliances. Then it will consider how a model for such an alliance has been developed in detail through my training of law enforcement hostage negotiators.

Many of the perceptions psychiatric and law enforcement groups have of one another depend on a well-worn set of prejudices. To some law enforcement professionals the psychiatrist is tender-hearted, mushy-minded, difficult to understand, and not much use in a "real" crisis. Psychiatrists, on the other hand, sometimes perceive police officers as quick on the trigger; possessed of practical common sense in human relationships but devoid of any real psychological sophistication. As with most prejudices, these beliefs set up their own vicious circle of expectations, differential treatment, and confirmation of the expectations.

In an effort to introduce some empirical data into this area, I conducted a research study that confronted both law enforcement and mental health professionals with decisions that might be involved in managing a hypothetical international terrorist hostage incident.

The subjects for this study were a group of 115 people—forty-nine mental health professionals and sixty-six police officers. The forty-nine psychiatric personnel were those attending a grand rounds presentation at the Temple University School of Medicine and included thirty-one psychiatrists, seven psychologists, seven student nurses, three medical students, and one social worker. The law enforcement group was composed of senior police officers attending a National Academy class at the FBI Academy of Quantico, Virginia. It is important to note that both the psychiatric and law enforcement groups were not selected on the basis of special training or interest in the field of terrorism or hostage negotiation. Both groups did have special background and training in their own professional disciplines. Thus, they represent the kinds of people who are likely to bear some of the operational responsibility for the resolution of local hostage incidents.

Law enforcement personnel would probably be the first group to respond in any terrorist or hostage incident. It should be acknowledged that this sample of law enforcement professionals was an elite group, since they had been chosen for a prestigious program of advanced training. These are the officers that would make the command-level decisions in a protracted hostage incident (in all likelihood, patrol officers, those who would respond initially to an evolving domestic-hostage situation, would have brought even less training to the hypothetical situations I presented). These police officers represent the raw material for any negotiator training program.

I will present the hypothetical situations first, so readers can decide which options they would choose. Then I will detail the choices the police and psychiatric groups made.

In the first situation, four political terrorists armed with automatic weapons and explosives have taken forty hostages. Two bystanders have been killed by the terrorists in the first few minutes of the incident. The hostages (twenty men, ten women, and ten children) are all native-born citizens and residents of your community. The terrorists (two men and two women) are making three demands. First, they want $1 million in cash. Second, they want ten members of their group who have been jailed in your country to be released and transported to a country that will accept them. These fellow terrorists have been convicted of murders that occurred in two similar past incidents. Third, they want a plane and pilot to fly *them* to a country willing to accept them. The terrorists have set a forty-eight-hour deadline and have threatened to, at the end of that deadline, begin killing one hostage per hour until all their demands are met.

The participants in the study were asked to assume that they were in a position to influence policy decisions in this incident. Readers are asked to do the same. The first question is, "Would you ask the media (TV, radio, and newspapers) to voluntarily suppress the incident until it is concluded?" Next, the participant must choose one of three options. Each option has been formulated with a probable outcome. The first option is to take no definitive action and allow the deadline to pass (with this option, there is a 50 percent probability that the terrorists will carry out their threat as stated). The second option is to attack with your special security force of thirty-five men and five women before the deadline expires (resulting in the probable death of two hostages, one member of the security force, and three terrorists, with the fourth terrorist wounded and captured alive). The final option is to grant all the terrorists' demands (your advisors believe that all hostages will be released at the terrorists' destination as promised). Participants were asked to rank these three options as their first (preferred), second, and third (least desirable) choices.

Since I was interested in studying emotional factors in decision making, I included a second case in the questionnaire. This second case contained the same set of options as the first, but applied them to a significantly different situation. It is unlikely that anyone would ever face this second situation in real life, but presenting it here does serve to measure how emotions can contribute to decisions made in hostage events. The second situation is the same as the first with one critical difference: Your spouse and child are among the hostages. Given these new facts, the participant is asked to consider and rerank the three response options of the first case to this situation.

Finally the participant is asked to decide on appropriate punishment for the terrorists. Specifically, the participant is asked to assume that the incident has been concluded and one of the terrorists has been captured, tried, and convicted of murder. The sentence can be either death or life imprisonment. The participant must decide between the two. Readers, whatever their professional background or involvement in the field of terrorism, may wish to take a few moments to answer these questions themselves before reading on.

The results of this empirical study show how wrong our preconceptions can be. Most of us would assume that suppression of the press, even when the press cooperates, would be a difficult issue to face even in the context of a terrorist event. In any case, many people would assume that law enforcement and psychiatric respondents would differ sharply along this dimension. In fact, the results were quite the opposite; 70 percent of the psychiatric group and 79 percent of the police officers supported suppression of the press. Although there is a 9 percent difference, this difference is not statistically significant. (Statistical significance in this study was determined by means of a four-cell chi-square determination for a dichotomized distribution.)

Only one of the three options—to delay and allow time to pass—would allow for possible negotiation. Both the assault and capitulation options in effect exclude a genuine negotiation process. Capitulation implies that a decision has already been made, and assault is incompatible with negotiation. This does not mean that both of these non-negotiation options cannot be applied in any given incident after delay and negotiation have failed. Of the psychiatric respondents, 33 percent chose the option of delaying. Of the police officers, 36 percent did the same, despite the fact that this group of police had not been specifically selected for training in hostage negotiation. The 3 percent difference, again, was not statistically significant. Many might be surprised by these similar responses, in view of the contemporary image of police as aggressive and active and psychiatrists as more passive and contemplative.

Of the psychiatric group, 51 percent favored an assault; 48 percent of the police did also. Many of the police officers probably based their choice of assault on some real-life experience with it. It is unlikely that any of the psychiatric respondents had any first-hand experience with this option, and those who chose it probably did so as a result of their exposure to it through television and movies.

How many of those who chose assault would do so even if their spouse and child were held hostage? If we consider only those subjects in each group who chose the assault option in the first case, 44 percent of the psychiatric group and 39 percent of the police officers said that under these new circumstances they would choose either the tactic of delaying or of capitulating. Again, there was no statistically significant difference between them.

This result carries an important message for us in terms of the influence of "human" factors on police and psychiatric decision making. Both groups, from different perspectives, are supposed to have these issues pretty well under control and to have dealt previously with the influence of personal factors on their professional decision making. One might assume that mental health professionals and police, by virtue of their training and experience, would have developed a certain "professional" objectivity to shield them from the sway of emotional influences. But it is clear from this result that a significant number of both psychiatrists and police officers acknowledge that they would be influenced by these human factors. I feel that this is a more encouraging response than the simple-minded "Once I've made up my mind, nothing would change it." I think that our society would have cause to be frightened if any professional group responded identically to *both* hypothetical situations.

Finally we come to punishment—the only area where there was a significant difference between the groups. Seventy percent of the psychiatric group favored the death penalty; so much for the preconception that psychiatrists are soft-hearted liberals. Ninety-three percent of the police officers favored the death penalty; the difference is statistically significant at the $p = .01$ level. Although I have no systematic data to explain this significant difference, several of the police officers in the experimental group made comments during later conversations such as "I know what happens in prison, what changes and what doesn't change." This contact police officers have with our penal system is just one hypothesis for explaining the difference in the data.

I have not presented all the data collected in the study. But the data I have presented do provide a perspective on how two different groups of helping professionals might handle the same kind of situation. There are more similarities than differences between the two groups, and these results may point the way to realistic possibilities for alliances between them.

Each professional group comes to this alliance with its

own background of experience and its own set of operational concepts and preconceptions. Some of these will foster the working alliance, others will make it more difficult. In the case of psychiatric professionals, the only group about whom I can speak first-hand, the major hindrances to the working alliance occur at a very basic level of role definition. Although many psychiatrists are able to take on a true consultant role when confronted with a complicated medical or surgical problem with psychosocial implications, this process of identifying oneself as a consultant and not as the ultimate decision maker is much more difficult when the problem itself is defined as within the psychosocial area.

There is a great tendency among psychiatrists when they are called into a psychological crisis to assume that they are the most educated, intelligent person in the decision making group and that they should either be in control or should have a crucial say in the decision making process. They assume that since they possess an understanding of the workings of the unconscious mind, they have the key to everything. Under these circumstances, if another member of the decision making group says that the psychiatrist does not know what he is talking about, the psychiatrist has the comforting tendency to interpret this as evidence that his critic is "too tightly defended" to realize he really doesn't know anything. This stance can be dangerous in many ways and is certainly one that isolates psychiatrists from helping and helpful relationships.

It is crucial for psychiatrists to recognize that in the United States the ultimate control and responsibility for the management of hostage situations will be in the law enforcement or military command structure. Usually, the police professional asks the psychiatrist a question to which he does expect an answer. But the police officer has no intention of giving up his authority. The psychiatrist's answer will usually be respected, but it may be respectfully disagreed with. That a psychiatric consultant's recommendation is not accepted does not mean that he did a bad job of offering advice. It means that the consultant's perspective was not the most useful one to those in command at the time. Events may prove both, or neither, parties to the consultant-consultee relationship right or wrong. Given the fact that a very high percentage (more than half by some estimates) of American hostage incidents involve persons with obvious mental disorder, a psychiatrist who is able to stay within the consultant relationship will have no trouble being relevant and needed in the resolution of many hostage situations.

If this relationship is to work, both parties must be prepared for it. Much of my own work has centered on preparing police officers who will be commanders or negotiators during hostage incidents to use the services of psychiatric consultants efficiently and accurately. I have attempted to accomplish this by introducing the police officers to a series of psychiatric concepts and perspectives that can be useful to them in conducting negotiations and in understanding when specialized help is needed. Such teaching and learning is best conducted in a small group or seminar format where participants have the opportunity to ask how general points relate to their particular work, and are encouraged to share their own experiences with hostage incidents with the group.

For most law enforcement officers a useful introduction to this area is a discussion of the broad range of basic types of psychiatric disorders. Each of these has some relevance to the hostage situation. I usually discuss situational reactions, neuroses (anxiety disorders), psychosomatic disorders, personality disorders, substance abuse problems, organic mental disorders, mood disorders, and the schizophrenias. A few words spent defining current concepts of each of these disorders help clear away prevalent misconceptions (that *schizophrenia* is a "split personality," for example) and provide a frame of reference for the participants. Neuroses and organic mental disorders do not play a major role in most hostage incidents. Criminal hostage-takers with personality disorders are not uncommon, but most police officers have skills in interviewing and managing these individuals equal to or better than those of the average psychiatrist. Concerning criminal hostage-takers, psychiatrists often learn from law enforcement personnel rather than vice versa.

Almost every hostage situation calls forth a clinically significant situational stress reaction for all those directly involved. The most well known situational reaction stemming from hostage situations is the Stockholm syndrome. This syndrome is still far from being completely explained and affords an excellent model for testing the operational relevance of various psychological explanatory schemes. Most law enforcement officers who have been trained in hostage negotiation are aware of this phenomenon and have thought out its practical implications.

Law enforcement officers, though, are often not as familiar with the influence of psychosomatic disorders (broadly defined as physical symptoms with emotional causes) on the conduct and outcome of hostage incidents. In fact, many common illnesses—including myocardial infarctions, asthma, hyperventilation, functional bowel or bladder disorders, diabetes mellitus, and various manifestations of muscular tension (especially where prolonged restraint or immobility is involved)—can be seriously exacerbated by the stresses of a hostage incident.

Knowledge of these psychosomatic conditions, even the most basic knowledge, leaves the hostage negotiator and law enforcement commander much better prepared to intervene helpfully in a hostage situation. A question such as "Does anyone in there have any medical problems that we should know about?" can often be the beginning of a life-affirming interaction between negotiator and hostage-taker that will undercut the murderous premise that can lead to fatal outcomes in hostage incidents. The problems of whether and how to send in medical help, or to insist that ill hostages be released, and the similar difficulties of dealing with intoxicated hostage-takers or with those who ask for mind-altering substances cannot be handled by simple prescriptive rules. These issues are best dealt with by discussing specific incidents (preferably drawn from the experience of the participants) and exploring relevant psychiatric concepts.

Although they usually are not classified as disorders, many "normal" physical functions have played a major role in determining the outcome of hostage incidents. Provisions for eating, drinking, sleeping, and toileting must be planned for in any hostage incident that lasts more than several hours. Providing, withholding, or manipulating facilities and supplies needed for each of these physiological functions affords valuable opportunities for those managing the incident to gather information, foster positive relationships, and, occasionally, even secure the release or escape of hostages. Detailed advance planning in this area is one of the crucial strategic advantages the well-prepared hostage negotiator can bring to an incident.

Within the mental health field, each professional discipline has its own special area of knowledge and expertise. For the psychiatrist, this area encompasses medical issues and those mental disorders that can best be seen as diseases. Two such diseases—psychotic (possibly suicidal) depressions and paranoid schizophrenia—account for much of what the hostage negotiator needs to learn from the psychiatrist. Both of these disorders can be thought of as illnesses that "happen" to someone who may have been healthy and functioning well previously. These diseases occur in all groups and strike poor, rich, virtuous, and evil alike.

A knowledge of the basic clinical symptoms of severe depression may be quite useful for a hostage negotiator. These symptoms include hopelessness, unrealistic feelings of guilt or worthlessness, slowed thinking, insomnia with early morning awakening, and suicidal thinking and behavior. Such symptoms can slow a hostage-taker's ability to make decisions, so negotiators who can spot them will know to be patient with the hostage-taker. Also, negotiators who possess this knowledge will be better able to predict how a hostage-taker will act. Perhaps most importantly, though, a familiarity with these symptoms will help negotiators establish a common ground between themselves and the hostage-taker. For example, a negotiator who asks a suicidally depressed hostage-taker if he has been having trouble sleeping, and in particular has been waking early, sometimes will get a "How did you know?" response. Thus the negotiator can, by demonstrating an intimate knowledge of the hostage-taker's problem, lay the foundation for a positive relationship. Negotiators can then tell the hostage-taker that they have seen these same symptoms in others, and that these "others" were subsequently treated successfully. Of course, negotiators should be familiar with modern methods for treating depression, which have been very successful in recent years.

The mentally ill hostage-taker suffering from paranoid schizophrenia may be even more frightening and difficult for law enforcement negotiators to handle. Unfortunately, negotiators cannot offer the same promise of successful treatment to them as they might to someone suffering from severe depression; the prognosis for treating paranoid schizophrenia is usually much more guarded. Moreover, it will be much more likely that the person will already have had contact with the psychiatric community. A naïve hostage negotiator might say something like "Joe, I know that you feel persecuted by the government and that radio waves have been affecting your body and the environment. This is what drove you to this situation. But we have Dr. Jones outside in the hall who'd like to talk to you; he's a psychiatrist and can help." This seems like a sensible approach. But the fact is that a paranoid schizophrenic hostage-taker will probably respond with something like: "Ah, yes. Jones. I remember him well; he sent me up for five years at the state hospital. Please send Dr. Jones in—I have something for him too." It may be, then, that such hostage-takers can form a more productive relationship with a law enforcement officer than with a psychiatrist. Of course, the psychiatrist can still play an extremely useful role as a consultant "behind the scenes." In any event, educating law enforcement negotiators in what the care system for the chronically psychotic patient is like will help prevent such unfortunate mistakes.

Law enforcement personnel can also gain useful insight as the psychiatrist discusses the features that characterize the behavior of persons with a paranoid delusional system (with or without hallucinations)—specifically their unusual concern for certain aspects of identity or autonomy (a concern with body space, for example, during an interview). Police officers are often skilled interviewers in usual circumstances, but some of the techniques most useful in dealing with psychotic persons are not intuitive. Many of these interviewing techniques psychiatrists do automatically, but this does not mean that they are unteachable. These special attitudes and behaviors, which the psychiatrist learns during residency training, can be communicated as specific skills; it is not necessary to teach police how to establish a long-term psychotherapeutic relationship. I have found it extremely helpful in this regard to use videotapes of interviews with severely depressed and paranoid patients to demonstrate the specifics of these techniques.

Another useful technique is that of role-playing. As part of the course offered for police negotiators at the FBI Academy, students spend one day at St. Elizabeth's Hospital in Washington, D.C., under the supervision of David Swink, the head of training in the psychodrama section. There they have the opportunity to role-play various situations that will come up in the course of hostage negotiation. In particular, this experience helps a negotiator determine how to deal with a hostage-taker who says something like, "You know they're sending those death rays at me, don't you?" For a negotiator confronting such an obviously deluded hostage-taker, there are several possible responses. It is tempting for the negotiator to try to be a "nice guy" and come back with a half-humorous response like, "Oh, yes, my radio is tuned to the same frequency." The psychotic hostage-taker may very well then reason that the negotiator must be crazy too and abandon the fragile bond of trust the negotiator has been trying to develop.

It is important to realize that the negotiator is attempting to form an alliance with the sane part of the psychotic person, a part that exists even in the most profoundly disturbed. This sane part of the person's personality, in fact, will be responsible for whatever rational action is possible on the hostage-taker's part. A better response to the above hostage-taker's initial statement, therefore, might be: "You know, I haven't received those radio waves myself. I know that people are very concerned with radiation from space these days and with its effects on the environment. I haven't had that experience, but I know that you have and that it is a very real experience for you that has brought you here. What I want to do is help you arrive at some resolution of this situation that will be OK for all of us."

It is important for the negotiator to have a chance during role-playing to practice this answer (or another similar one that is more comfortable) so that it feels natural, rather than waiting for a real-life situation to try it. What is involved here is refining a response that will be natural for the negotiator. Something that works for one person may not work for another; a cookbook approach has no place in this field. It is this opportunity for practice and refinement that leaves the negotiator better prepared after training than before.

Whatever their professional and personal orientations, most people in charge of hostage situations share one perferred outcome: that in which all participants—hostages, hostage-takers, law enforcement personnel, and observers—emerge from the incident alive and unhurt. However, people can and do argue about which of the several other less optimal outcomes are preferrable. For example, are the lives of children worth more than the lives of older people? What about the hostage-taker who has already executed hostages—is his life still worth saving? Does the professional role of law enforcement officers make it more permissible for them to take greater risks? This kind of calculus is difficult to contemplate and dangerous to deal with in the hostage situation. But, consciously or unconsciously, these decisions are made. So there is likely some room for useful empirical research on how these decisions are reached in actual hostage situations. Nevertheless, we can still define a basic standard: The outcome is best when no one is killed; the more people killed, the worse the outcome. Thus the opportunity to manage these situations successfully is seen as an opportunity to avoid unnecessary killing. If our interventions as negotiators, commanders, or consultants are successful, this is how their success can be measured.

Hostage-taking has become an endemic disorder of our day. Whether politically, criminally, or psychopathologically motivated, these incidents challenge our strength to do, and to abstain from doing. No philosophical or political perspective seems adequate to deal with them successfully and humanely at the same time. It has been useful for me, though, to recall the words of Thomas Jefferson: In 1774, as he struggled to summarize the actual assets that free people possess even in the face of an impending serious conflict, he said: "The God who gave us life, gave us liberty at the same time: The hand of force may destroy, but cannot disjoin them." I think that is a very important concept. As long as people are alive, even in the most constrained and difficult situations, they have some liberty left, some ability to make decisions.

For me, one of the most important challenges in teaching people about hostage situations is that law enforcement officers (and sometimes psychiatrists) called into these situations have often felt trapped and without any meaningful decisions to make, just as the hostages and hostage-takers feel trapped. The history of successful efforts by psychiatric and law enforcement personnel to work together in the field of hostage negotiation has been the history of our discovery that we have much more liberty to make decisions, much more potency to influence the outcome, than we had thought. This potency does not always have to do with the use of violent counterforce; strength can be quiet and kind.

The many former hostages who are alive today testify to the effectiveness of this approach—those who are not testify to what remains to be learned and to be done. The law enforcement personnel who serve as negotiators in the United States have been open to the meaningful contributions of psychiatry in this area. As a psychiatrist who has endeavored to teach them, I have little trouble identifying the most important source of whatever help I have been able to offer. It was best expressed long ago by Rabbi Judah ha-Nasi when he said "I learned much from my teachers, more from my colleagues, and most of all from my students."

Part Four

Research in Terrorism

Research in Terrorism

Introduction

WILLIAM REID, M.D., M.P.H.

I shall add only a few pages to the foregoing work. Much of what is contained in this volume has been reported research. Some of it is retrospective, some prospective; some anecdotal and some very well structured although observational. Dr. Symonds is well known for his elegant interpretations of rich clinical material. Special Agent Hassel and Captain Bolz have culled the social sciences and their own experience in an effort to develop management techniques appropriate to each. The authors of the ethics section have drawn upon the human experience to share with us what they feel civilization has found to work best for the ongoing societal good. Mr. Jenkins' chapter, which follows, brings much information about the perpetrator and his constituency, although the data-gathering abilities of even the Rand Corporation are hampered by the difficulties inherent in the topic.

Less with us during the meeting that gave rise to this volume—and conspicuous in their absence—have been the kinds of data that scientists most like to see. There is a real dearth of blind studies, or even of those with rigid observational controls. Some of our lack of knowledge is related to this deficit, some to primitive or nonexistent technology, and some to the ubiquitous specter of dwindling social and fiscal support.

Some research problems may be related to the need for different disciplines to work together and the reluctance of some professionals to engage in what Henrik Blum has called "boundary crossing."[1] Perhaps our differences are not so great as often thought; psychiatrists, statesmen, and police may have more similarities than is outwardly apparent.

Some difficulties arise from our moral constraints. One could study almost anything more effectively if he weren't limited when studying human beings. We do not carry out unannounced mock raids on world communities. We don't experiment with kidnapping different groups of school children and we don't deny the human rights of even the most heinous perpetrator, at least not in the name of research.

Research into the group dynamics and infrastructure of terrorist organizations has been conducted in greatest detail by J. K. Zawodny.[2] His writing, which reflects the experience and point of view of a social scientist and national security consultant, offers rare insights into the personal and political motives of the terrorist.

Also missing in this volume, and rare in the literature in general, is a look into biochemical or physiologic data. This has partly to do with the lack of conclusive results at this time, and partly to do with the absence from this volume of those engaged in this kind of work. While one must first identify the many different kinds of terrorists and any gross characteristics that make them more visible for study, there are areas in which technology may be ready for those kinds of microscopic examinations when and if they are called for.[3-5]

At present, I am involved in collaborative work at the Nebraska and Illinois Psychiatric Institutes on possible neurochemical correlates of severe antisocial syndromes and on the treatment of some of them.[6] These and other projects within related fields may well have disappointing results, as with the psychophysiological studies of the 1950s and 1960s, in which important information emerged but clinically useful results fell short of what had been promised to, or expected by, the scientific and political communities. One hopes that those results and the methodology that was developed in obtaining them will find more usefulness as time goes by. Whether the terrorist himself will be seen to have been addressed by our work is too much an extrapolation of our data, given the current state of the art in this field.

There is a sort of conceptual similarity between some points in Mr. Jenkins' chapter and Professor Kaplan's earlier sensing of what he called the birth pangs of a new stage of development for psychiatry or medicine. Historically, both the need for and the availability of the means to allay discomfort have guided the physician's setting of criteria for medical progress. Initially there was a concentration on the organ and on the search for nonspiritual etiology of disease. Later, the organism itself was found to contribute to its failings through heredity and behavior. Now, the "whole person" is studied and treated as the "mind-body continuum," and forays are made into the ills of the community and society. Perhaps we are indeed gathered up in an evolution of human understanding.

If so, then I think that Dr. Soskis has pointed out some things of great importance in his chapter. Such an evolution remains a ponderous movement, and not one in which an individual psychiatrist, sociologist, or any other single person plays a crucial role. Except in some special, usually profit-motivated instances—and profit is used here in a broad sense—serious research comes along later in movements such as this. It is not ordinarily seen as useful or cost-effective by those in positions of influence, and there are few philanthropies that will support such endeavors until the hour is past. We all share the hope that this is not going to be the case in the field of terrorism.

REFERENCES

1. Blum H: *Planning for Health: Development and Application of Social Change Theory.* New York: Human Sciences Press, 1974.
2. Zawodny JK: Internal organizational problems and the sources of tensions of terrorist movements as catalysts of violence. *Terrorism: An International Journal* 1:277–285, 1977.
3. Elliott FA: Neurological aspects of antisocial behavior. In *The Psychopath: A Comprehensive Study of Antisocial Disorders and Behaviors.* Edited by Reid WH. New York: Brunner/Mazel, 1978.
4. Hare RD, Cox DN: Psychophysiological research on psychopathology. In *The Psychopath: A Comprehensive Study of Antisocial Disorders and Behaviors.* Edited by Reid WH. New York: Brunner/Mazel, 1978.
5. Eysenck HJ, Eysenck SBG: Psychopathy, personality and genetics. In *Psychopathic Behavior: Approaches to Research.* Edited by Hare RD, Schalling D. London: John Wiley and Sons, 1978.
6. Reid WH (ed): *The Treatment of Antisocial Syndromes.* New York: Van Nostrand Reinhold, 1981.

9

Research in Terrorism: Areas of Consensus, Areas of Ignorance

BRIAN JENKINS, Ph.D.

As an historian, I am inclined to look at recent events in the context of broader historical trends or movements. In that light, it is interesting to note that right now, September 1979, we are less than four months from the end of what some may call "the decade of the terrorist." To be sure, there were wars during the 1970s: guerrilla wars, civil wars, full-scale military wars. There have been mad bombers, mass murders, and even mass suicides. It was the terrorist, though, that dominated the headlines of the era.

As one looks back upon the 1970s, almost every year is characterized by a single event, a single individual, or one or two striking terrorist incidents that captured our imaginations and in many cases provoked enormous alarm. In 1970, three airliners were hijacked and flown to Dawson Field in Jordan. The spectacle of the airliners sitting on the desert airstrip, the several hundred hostages surrounded by Palestinian terrorists who in turn were surrounded by Jordanian security forces, and the complex negotiations between governments and the terrorists were reported to us in detail through television cameras as the weeks went by before the last of the hostages were released.

In 1971 there was a spate of kidnappings in Latin America. The most striking, perhaps, was that of Geoffrey Jackson, the British ambassador to Uruguay, who was held for nine months in a wire cage in an underground "peoples' prison" of the Tupamaros.

The watershed year was 1972. Two particularly shocking incidents acted as catalysts for a number of governments, including that of the United States, to devote more serious attention to the problem of terrorism and to begin to deal with it in an organized fashion. In May 1972, Japanese terrorists trained in North Korea and the Middle East boarded an aircraft in Europe, debarked at Israel's Lod airport, and began machine-gunning the other passengers, most of whom, ironically, were Puerto Rican pilgrims on their way to the Holy Land; pilgrims killed in the name of the Palestinian liberation movement—a truly international incident. Shortly thereafter, in September, came the Munich tragedy.

In 1973, two American diplomats were held hostage and murdered in the Saudi Arabian embassy in Khartoum. The year 1974 saw the Palestinian-claimed bombing of a TWA airliner in which eighty-eight people were killed, and the takeover of the French embassy at The Hague by members of the Japanese Red Army. The year 1975 captured the world's attention as the year of Carlos, the year of OPEC. In 1976, the most striking event was the hijacking of an Air France jetliner to Uganda and the daring Israeli rescue at Entebbe.

The Schleyer kidnapping and the rescue of the hostages at Mogadishu stood out in 1977; 1978 was the year of Italy, the year of Moro's kidnapping and murder. And the year 1979? Certainly the assassination of Lord Mountbatten, with its accompanying apparent resurgence of IRA terrorism, was the most heinous event.

Through such acts, small groups of political extremists have demonstrated that by using terrorist tactics they can achieve a disproportionate effect on the world. They have been able to call attention to themselves and to their causes. They have been able to provoke worldwide alarm. They have been able to cause government crises, frequently international crises. They have compelled governments to devote increasing resources and attention to security against their attacks.

ATTEMPTS TO STUDY THE PROBLEM

Conferences and Literature

With the rapid increase in acts of terrorism during the 1970s, particularly in Western Europe, there has been a growth of scientific literature dealing with the topic. The research and academic communities have focused greater attention than ever on a number of areas.

An international conference on terrorism was held during 1978 in Berlin, at which John Wykert noted that there were some fifty terrorist groups active in the world at that time, with a total membership of about 3,000 (U.S. Department of Justice figures). Of these, only a small number of groups, with a total of about 200 hard-core members, have carried out the major international actions. Wykert calculated that since sixty international experts attended the Berlin conference, it seemed that there was one expert to every three-and-one-third terrorists.*

In fact, considerable research has been done on the topic and there is a growing body of relevant literature that includes a quarterly journal dedicated to the subject of terrorism. Not surprisingly, the countries most affected by terrorist acts have led in research efforts. These include West Germany, Italy, Israel, the United Kingdom, Holland, and the United States. Available information would indicate that relatively little research has been done in Spain and not much more in Latin America. France has addressed the topic of terrorism tangentially within the field of criminology; however, to my knowledge (which may be lacking) little else is being done.

Scholarly exchange of views has taken place at meetings such as that held in Baltimore and at large international conferences like the ones in Evian, Berlin, and Tel Aviv. There is a kind of informal, international network of scholars and government officials with interests or responsibilities in the area of terrorism. A kind of "college-without-campus" has emerged. This is an extremely useful development for two reasons. First, it facilitates exchange of information both during the conferences and later as a result of contacts made between professionals. Second, these gatherings allow for greater review by one's peers in a critical setting than has tended to be the case in past research on terrorism.

The conventional wisdom about new journals in any field is that one way to tell whether a field has successfully established itself as a scholarly effort is to observe the han-

---

*Wykert J: A meeting on terrorism. *Psychiatric News*, April 20, 1979, p 1.

dling of manuscripts. When the rejections by the journal begin to exceed the number of articles accepted, one may infer that a sufficient number of people have begun to look at things critically and have sufficient exchange of information for objective critique.

I think we are just beginning to enter that stage in the field of terrorism. There has not been enough critical review of other works and no real attempts have been made to judge what is purported to have been done. Up to now the area of terrorism has been a sort of small hopper into which many things have been tossed by a lot of people. Frivolous and nonsensical things have been mixed with some good work. Bowyer Bell has noted that research on terrorism is "largely a cottage industry." It is at least true that for the most part such work has been a collection of individual efforts, either by persons in government with a particular interest in terrorism, or by individuals in research or academic communities.

National Efforts

There are, however, a few larger group efforts that deserve mention. The West Germans have launched the most ambitious research drive in the field of terrorism. A project is currently underway on the causes of terrorist activity, for which approximately two million deutsche Mark have been allocated. It is intended to be an exhaustive and thorough inquiry aimed at closing gaps in our knowledge of terrorism.

The project has four parts. The first is an analysis of terrorists' lives. Biographical and social data have been collected about the members of terrorist groups; so far, an enormous quantity of data has been acquired. German investigators now want to do some multivariate analyses for symptoms. One of the specific topics of investigation is evidence of "progressive inhibition reduction." This concept is an imperfect translation of a marvelous and very long German word and represents quite an interesting area of inquiry.

The second part of the study is an examination of group formation and processes. Leadership recruitment, organization, and internal group dynamics will be studied. The Germans have referred to an entity best described as "group compulsion." That is, do terrorist groups have an inner need for action in order to stay alive, to train new members, or perhaps to recruit new members? Do they have to keep up a separate level of internal activity apart from external conditions?

The third area of the German study deals with social conditions that may be conducive to terrorism. Project write-ups note a similarity between German, Italian, and Japanese terrorist activities. This finding has led to a number of hypotheses about the relationship between terrorism and governments that have undergone a sharp ideological break with either an authoritarian or fascist past, raising the question of the legitimacy of the various kinds of democratic systems in these countries.

Finally, ideological influences and cross-national comparisons are being addressed. This is a multidisciplinary effort, heavy in data and heavily quantitative thanks to modern computer techniques. One can't be quite sure what the results will be, but they should be interesting.

The Italians also have done considerable research, both inside and outside the government, largely as a result of reaction to the Red Brigades and other terrorist groups. The work tends to be heavily sociological, but there are a number of parallels to the West German study, particularly in their efforts to develop life histories of those in terrorist groups, both leftist and rightist. These data will be subjected to very elaborate multivariate analyses in order to try to develop conclusions about the kinds of individuals who are attracted to such groups. We shall return to that issue a bit later.

Israel, not surprisingly, has been a center of research in terrorism. A number of scholars at various universities and in affiliation with the government are engaged in such work. The focus is largely on the Palestinian issue, but there is also investigation into strategic and policy questions that have been of great interest to the Israelis.

Research in the United States tends to reflect the source of most of its funding—the government. Much of the work is very pragmatic, and tends toward subjects related to either national policy or law enforcement. There has been little government funding for basic research, which I find regrettable. Dr. Ochberg earlier mentioned the desire of individuals such as ourselves to advance the frontiers of knowledge. It is, however, very hard to find a government official with a limited budget who is interested in advancing the frontiers of knowledge. These officials and the agencies they represent are far more interested in solving specific problems. Thus most research is of the problem-solving type, often narrowly defined, and dedicated, for example, to police training, the handling of certain kinds of cases, the role of international law, the application of technology, or the development of security at vital facilities. The government client in each case does not want to know why people become terrorists, how terrorists behave, or whether they are psychotic or nonpsychotic. What he wants to know is: How many of them are coming? Will they have submachine guns or not? How high should the fence be? To be sure, in addressing some of these issues, some basic research is done. A small share of the problem-solving money can be siphoned informally into areas of more basic work.

As closely directed as research on terrorism has been, still one may reasonably criticize some rather frivolous study ideas that may have received funding. Terrorism seems to be a subject that lends itself to a "black box" scheme in which the study rationale is sometimes less than clear.

Those are the characteristics of the national efforts. The topics that have been addressed overall, speaking internationally again, reflect the fact that terrorism is a problem of many dimensions and many disciplines. Much of the work already done can be placed in the category of broad, interpretive description, combining history, current events, theory, and political points of view.

CAUSES OF TERRORISM

The etiology of terrorism has received much attention. Specifically, the sociocultural determinants and specific conditions that might lead to terrorist-prone societies have been of interest. Many hypotheses have arisen, some of which have quickly become ideological. In the last analysis, however, it is still unknown whether terrorism is a violent expression of legitimate grievances, the only form of struggle available to dissidents in societies, an alternative means of bringing pressure upon a repressive government, or even the natural by-product of a free society. It is interesting to note that very little terrorism is seen in totalitarian countries, leading some to consider the possibility that terrorism is a product of freedom, particularly of freedom of the press. In a related way, some feel that the disparate levels of terrorism in Western democracies (compared with Eastern bloc countries) may reflect active Soviet or other Communist support for terrorism in the West.

Proponents of historical origins for terrorism quickly note that many such movements reflect unresolved ideological differences, ethnic divisions, or peculiar political paths within countries and governments. For example, the three former members of the Axis—Japan, Germany, and Italy—each seemed to spawn a particular brand of terrorism in the 1970s.

Other hypotheses suggest economic, social, and demographic factors such as sudden increases in university populations in certain countries. The development of data bases has thus far been insufficient to explore these fully.

OTHER AREAS OF INQUIRY

Hostage Situations

Another area of inquiry has to do with dealing with hostage situations. Unlike other research topics, this area tends to be highly empirical, drawing from a great deal of actual experience and case studies. There is considerable international sharing of results, some of which are presented in this volume. Data available as a result of the continuing occurrence of incidents, unfortunate as that may be, have led to far greater understanding of the field of hostage situations, making it an exception to the highly theoretical nature of inquiries in other areas of the subject of terrorism.

Victimology

The second exception is research in victimology. The victims of terrorism have attracted much scholarly interest among psychiatrists and psychologists. This is an area rich in data, with a solid base of interviews, psychiatric evaluations, and so on.

Most of this research has focused on the victims of hostage incidents. It may also be possible to devote some attention to victims of other kinds of terrorist events; for example, survivors of bombings. I recently spoke with several persons who had survived bombings. With vivid recall, they spoke of a marked slowing of events during the split second of the actual detonation of the bomb, much as in a very slow motion movie. In addition, victims of various kinds of maimings, such as "kneecapping" in leg shootings in Italy, might be studied. Anecdotal accounts indicate that many of the men who have been victims of kneecapping have suffered deep psychological problems, impotence, and other kinds of continuing disabilities that may be related to the sudden, violent assault on their legs.

As has been pointed out, it is useful to think of all society as victims. There is a first-order level such as victims of hijackings and their immediate families. Over the years, the total population of such individuals has begun to approach a fairly sizable number. That is, a significant number of people, either first-hand or very close second-hand (through a relative), have been touched by a victim experience. Many of these people either bear grudges or develop certain attitudes about their government's ability to protect people. They may be outwardly hostile to the government's apparent lack of responsiveness to their problems during and after the episode. The notion of a large population of victims is something worth examining, especially when we think of the kinds of people who often become hostages—diplomats, business executives, and journalists. This is a fairly articulate portion of the population, people who are accustomed to speaking their mind or writing papers or articles for newspapers. To what extent are they shaping the attitudes of the general public?

News Media

The role of the news media has attracted a tremendous amount of interest and has been the topic of several conferences. A number of studies have been devoted to discovering the important interaction between mass communication and terrorism. Various aspects have been examined, including a search for direct relationships between the number of incidents and the number of newspaper column inches or network minutes devoted to terrorist activity. The recurrence of similar kinds of terrorist incidents following (and apparently related to) particularly graphic reporting makes some people believe there is a statistical correlation between the two, although such an assumption may be unwarranted. There has yet to be an adequate explanation of society's appetite for vicarious violence and of the relationship between the audience, the victim, and the events. We need to explore further the dynamics of the interactions between the content, method of presentation, and audience.

One broad area of study can be described as prescriptive in terms of security measures, government organization, and government policy. This literature generally reflects the fact that terrorists can cause a major diversion of resources to various kinds of security measures and functions, sometimes creating paralyzing crises at the top level of national leadership in a country.

International law is another major area of research. Still another has to do with the possibility that terrorists may begin to use nuclear weapons or other instruments of mass murder, a possibility that has caused great, perhaps exaggerated concern. Thus far terrorists have achieved their limited goals of publicity and coercion without resorting to such measures.

Casualties

Only about 34 percent of international terrorist incidents have any physical casualties at all. If one adds local acts of terrorism—those occurring within the borders of a single country such as Italy, France, Germany, or the United States and involving only local residents—the percentage of those with casualties drops still further. The low casualty rate primarily is related to the fact that local terrorism includes more token acts of violence, such as small bombs placed in front of embassies in the middle of the night. The modal number of casualties per incident is one, adding to an overall total that is minuscule compared with the world volume of violence. Of course, one should not be nonchalant about the death of any individual, but if one looks at terrorism in terms of the total number of casualties, then it is easy to see the extent to which the terrorists have created tremendous effects in the world with relatively minor bloodshed.

Since 1968 fewer than 2,000 people have been killed in international terrorist incidents. If we add domestic terrorism in places like Belfast or Buenos Aires, the total rises to somewhere around 10,000 or more. Compare this figure with, say, the annual homicide rate in the United States, which is on the order of 20,000 a year. Measured against the number of people killed in wars, this number becomes even smaller, since in the thirteen wars that have taken place in the world since 1968, several million people have lost their lives. Compared with the great wars, World Wars I and II, the significance shrinks by another factor of ten.

When some members of the older generation shake their heads and complain of the violence of the present world, they seem to forget that the past was much more violent. This fact has led to a hypothesis that terrorism may be the price we pay for peace; that is, wars have a way of absorbing some of the people who might otherwise go into terrorist activities. Thus, one way of getting rid of terrorism may be to have a major war and assume that the lesser volume of potential terrorist violence will be consumed by it. It is an interesting hypothesis, but one that is difficult to test.

The point to be made is that, thus far, there have been relatively few casualties per terrorist incident, and comparatively few overall, a fact that cannot be explained entirely in terms of technical constraints on the terrorist. I shall not address the question of whether terrorists possess the capabilities to obtain and/or construct nuclear weaponry, but certainly they have the technical skills and organizational abilities necessary for acquiring and using, say, powerful chemical weapons. They have demonstrated their capability to use even conventional explosives or the deadly instrument of fire in ways that can kill large numbers of people. If terrorists really wanted to get into the killing business, it is clear that they could.

My view is that in general terrorists want a lot of people watching, not a lot of people dead. They may view mass murder as counterproductive since such acts may alienate those perceived as constitutents, provoke backlash, and permit the government to crack down on even those groups and causes that may be popular with the public. In addition, large-scale killings might cause debate and dissension within the ranks of the terrorist organization itself, thus exposing the operation and the organization to betrayal from within.

By the same token, there is some agreement among those who spend much time watching the phenomenon of terrorism that the most important terrorist groups in the world are at some kind of critical juncture. That is, they have achieved just about all they can expect to achieve using the tactics they have used to date. Another bombing, another hijacking will not get them much more; indeed, it is likely to get them less. As Frank Bolz pointed out in his chapter, governments are becoming increasingly sophisticated and resistant to the demands of terrorists, even when large numbers of hostages are involved, and increasingly some are willing to resort to force when necessary (see, for example, Professor Kaplan's discussion of Israeli policy).

This response applies to international terrorist incidents, not nonpolitical criminal events in which there is not an increasing use of force but an increasing use of negotiation. In the large international incidents, the Mogadishus, the Entebbes, the Luxors, and so on there is an increasing willingness to use violence when necessary and to end such episodes despite the obvious risks to the hostages. This stance has proved popular with the general public, especially in countries fraught with fear of terrorism and in countries like Israel, where such incidents are considered acts of war.

Thus there appears to be a popular mandate for resistance to terrorist demands and for the use of force when necessary. One must say, of course, that these feelings have been affected by the splendid luck and spectacular successes at Entebbe and Mogadishu. Had those operations been disasters where half the hostages were killed, the world view of that type of intervention might be entirely different.

The publicity value of terrorist episodes has also been declining. The first hijacking is page one news; the second, page two; and unless it involves special conditions a hijacking today may end up back on page 17. This declining news value is also a result of the long-range effects of media coverage. We tend to lament the fact that the media coverage given to any single event inflates that event. It does, of course, inflate the seeming importance of the single event; but it goes on to work in much the way as economic inflation: if inflation continues, then ultimately the value of the currency—in this case the terror created by the terrorist—loses value. The same act repeated ad nauseam begins to have declining publicity value.

If the observers of this phenomenon are indeed correct and terrorists are at a critical juncture, then what will they do next? Will they fade to extinction on the back pages of newspapers? Will they go on as they have for years, for reasons other than those readily discernible to outside observers? Will they escalate into new areas of violence?

One's conclusions about what terrorists are most likely to do next depend in large measure upon knowing something about the terrorist "mindset" and the terrorist decision making process. If we judge that people who join terrorist groups are those who tend to be easily disillusioned with society, then a logical next step is to consider the possibility that those same persons may also become disillusioned with terrorism and drop out. One might speculate that this is what happened in the cases of Hans Klein and "Bommi" Bauman, two West German terrorists who have dropped out of their movements.

On the other hand, might they simply go on with what they are doing because they are largely inner-driven? That is, do they derive some kind of personal satisfaction from a bombing, a kidnapping, or a hijacking, or in being a member of an underground organization? Are the members attracted to lives of danger, intrigue, and the possibility of occasionally exploding onto the world scene and becoming for a moment the center of world attraction? If so, there is little need for them to change, because they are satisfied that terrorism works; that is, it works for them. Long-term measures of success or failure have less meaning within this model.

Or will they go on doing as they have simply because they are the kind of people who are totally unreceptive, unsusceptible to external influences? Such persons may have a very rigid mindset, and therefore loss of support or public backlash would have very little effect on their activities. This question is important for police in some parts of the world, and for the policy of certain governments that debate whether there is any way to rehabilitate terrorists. Disillusionment might open a path back for some, but for those incapable of disillusionment, there may be no way out of a terrorist group short of death or capture. This fact raises questions about the effectiveness of attempts to offer limited amnesties. For them, will there ever be any way back in?

AREAS OF CONSENSUS

Distribution

Out of all of this research, a few areas of consensus have emerged. The uneven distribution of terrorism throughout the world is easily demonstrated; a handful of nations experience a disproportionate amount of the world's terrorism. About twenty countries account for between 75 to

90 percent of all reported incidents, international and domestic. Of all terrorist activity, 58 to 72 percent takes place within ten countries, a striking statistic.

For the countries that recur within the "top ten," their order shifts from time to time and one or two may drop below the "ten" slot on occasion. Those that appear again and again are Italy, France, Spain, Germany, the United Kingdom, Greece, the United States, Turkey, Israel, Argentina, and Colombia. Even when one adjusts for events with casualties and for local versus international incidents, the same countries appear at the top.

This unequal distribution can be explained in part by biases in reporting incidents. Countries in which there is a high frequency of incidents may be over-represented because the press in those countries reports many smaller acts. Countries in which the press is controlled by the government tend to be under-represented. There seems no easy way of getting around the issue of under-reporting in countries that have a state-controlled press.

Another bias in the reporting system is the fact that urban violence tends to be heavily reported; there seems to be far less terrorism going on in rural areas. Perhaps this appears true because rural areas offer fewer lucrative targets since they usually are not centers of corporate headquarters, government facilities, communications industries, and other vulnerable targets that terrorists often choose to exploit. On the other hand, at a village level there may be a great deal of terrorism that, although lacking some of the technological sophistication of urban forays, is terrorism nonetheless.

Much terrorism takes place in one country but is directed against another. For example, when the Israeli embassy in Bangkok, Thailand, is the target of an attack, Israel is clearly the country being terrorized. An adjustment must also be made for countries that are locations but not targets of attack. It is interesting to note here that the Soviet Union, Cuba, and Yugoslavia appear well down the list of political targets and locations.

There is little or no consensus on the reasons why certain countries, primarily Western ones, are the usual targets of terrorism. Liberal democracies have comparably high per capita gross national products and are largely urban. Many theories have been profferred about sociocultural determinants, but these quickly become ideological, with one end of the spectrum seeing the Western countries as targets of Eastern plots and the other end blaming such problems on the "sick" Western societies.

Modern Society

There is general agreement that a relationship exists between modern terrorism and modern society. Evidence of the relationship remains even after allowing for the reporting bias mentioned above. Much of the kind of terrorism that has attracted our attention depends on technological advances. Modern jet travel has provided terrorists with worldwide mobility as well as a source of targets. Increased availability of weapons and explosives leads to increased capacity for violence. The vulnerability of facilities like nuclear plants, and the public attention that is focused on them, is another example of a technological advance that serves as a target.

Mass Communications

There is consensus that mass communication, specifically the news media, is an essential ingredient in terrorism. This is especially true if by terrorism we mean the entire domain of acts carried out by terrorists, their effects on society, and society's reactions. Because of the essential link provided by the news media, there has been a strong interest in how terrorist incidents are handled, or should be handled, by the press. Unfortunately, the agreement often ends there. Some observers charge that the news media inspire acts of terrorism or are often willing accomplices of the terrorists. A less hostile view is that mass communication is responsible for terrorism to about the same extent that civil aviation is responsible for hijackings. One can stop hijacking by grounding all civil aircraft; perhaps terrorism could be reduced by complete media blackouts. We cannot do this, however; access to information is a vulnerability inherent in a modern free society and the issue must be dealt with in that context.

Hostage Situations

There are many areas of consensus here, most of which are supported by empirical evidence and research. The issues of perpetrators, victims, and hostage situations are admirably discussed elsewhere in this volume.

Prognosis

Lastly, there is consensus that terrorism will persist in international society. The verb "persist" is chosen with some care, in order to avoid predictions such as "increase" or "decrease." Over the past ten years there has been a general drifting upward of the number of terrorist incidents. Part of this increase has been due to more complete recording and reporting, but even after adjusting for this there is an upward drift.

A look at the past 150 years of Western civilization shows that political violence in one form or another has been a pretty permanent feature—terrorism is only the latest manifestation. The burden of proof thus seems to be more on those who say "this will go away" than on those who say "if we allow for the locus of violence and its modes to change, terrorism will persist in one form or another."

AREAS OF IGNORANCE

We have devoted a great deal of attention to studying the organization, financing, weaponry, and tactics of terrorist groups. We have acquired a great deal of what might be called "order of battle" information about such organizations. In some cases a sizable portion of their membership has been identified. We know their names. Articles, and in some cases books, have been written about a few of the more notable leaders, some of whom have written about their own experiences. Some terrorists in prison have agreed to be interviewed, and some still at large have given "underground" audiences to journalists. There is still, however, insufficient information on which to base realistic predictions about terrorist "profiles" or about the methods of decision making that are used within terrorist groups.

Terrorist "Profiles"

On the basis of information about apprehended or identified members of terrorist groups, we have been able to construct a kind of demographic profile of the typical terrorist. The pioneering work was done by Dr. Charles Russell.

The typical terrorist is male, although there are many exceptions; in fact, 60 percent of the Baader-Meinhoff terrorists were women. But, overall, we see people who are males in their early 20s, unmarried, from middle- or up-per-class families, well educated (although often university dropouts), who most frequently joined or were recruited into the group while at a university. There are exceptions, such as the Irish Republican Army, in which the members tend to come from lower socioeconomic sectors.

A more speculative attempt at finding common psychological characteristics describes the terrorist as absolutist. Such people are "true believers," who may switch ideologies but who will always passionately cling to whichever one they follow at the moment. They tend to be uncompromising and prone to seek instant gratification through their actions. They often are "gun freaks." It is interesting to note, for example, that the favorite reading of the West German terrorists was not Marx, Lenin, Marighella, or Mao Tse-tung, but gun magazines. In some cases there appears to be abnormal fascination with firearms and explosives. Hostages have spoken about the behavior of political terrorists with their firearms; the constant cleaning and fondling of weapons, and the endless discussions of ammunition and like suggest obsession.

Such individuals generally are not suicidal, but might be described as risk-seekers since they apparently are willing to court death, possibly to impress peers. One psychiatrist has stated that the terrorist suffers from anonymity, deprivation, and a sense of powerlessness, and feels his self-esteem and masculinity have been consistently assaulted. The same psychiatrist feels that through acts of terrorism the individuals may seek not only attention but intimacy with the powerful figures of society. Although there is little empirical evidence to support this belief, there is little to support other hypotheses, and I would agree with the logic of the statement.

Thus, despite all of the speculations, we cannot say with confidence that we have penetrated the terrorist's mind. We do not know why a politically or socially disaffected person goes underground, takes up arms, and declares war on society—a total war that allows no innocent bystanders. We do not know whether this transformation is a result of individual predisposition or is largely circumstantial. How does a person who is socially or politically disaffected and willing to be violent ultimately make contact with a terrorist group? Is it circumstantial, or is there a way that these people are funneled down a path that inevitably puts them in the line of a group recruiting effort? The answers to these questions are crucial to the understanding of organized terrorism.

Are there born terrorists? Are there those who are predisposed to the kinds of behavior described in the preceding pages? We do not know at this point whether terrorists in general suffer from some common psychosis, or from any psychosis at all. Wilfried Rasch, a psychiatrist who has had the opportunity to observe and interview many of Germany's terrorists, believes they do not. We do not know whether there is a common terrorist personality or a common mindset—that is, a common perspective, point of view, or way of looking at the world and at one's own identity relative to other persons and things.

We don't know whether terrorists undergo some common radicalizing experience. Political circumstances alone seem to offer an inadequate explanation for terrorist behavior. Thousands of individuals may go through similar political and social frustrations, and may go through similar radicalizing experiences, but only a handful become terrorists. Why? Are these random human events circumstantial, or is there some previous disposition?

There are also a number of physiological hypotheses on the cause of terrorist behavior, ranging from inner-ear malfunction to diet deficiencies. Although the validity of each of these is difficult to ascertain, further research and more convincing statistics, subject to peer review, may make the physiological approach more persuasive than it is at the present time. A note of caution is necessary. Observers of terrorist activity, as well as terrorists' audiences, are highly receptive to the notion that there is some overall physiological or psychological explanation for terrorism. The labeling of terrorists as "sick" persons, as being mentally or physically impaired in some way, has great appeal to those who would prefer not to face the fact that social, economic, and political injustices exist in the world. The grievances that terrorists claim to express—which is not to imply that such grievances justify their actions— can be denied by simply seeing these people as "sick." In such a system we don't have to worry about ourselves; it's them. Even if clusters of behavioral traits common to most terrorists can be identified, or if personality types predisposed to terrorist activity can be defined, these findings should not prevent us from recognizing contributing political or social problems.

A great deal more research is needed in the area of the terrorist mindset. More data are needed, more exchange of data must take place, and indirect techniques of analysis must be developed.

Terrorist Decision Making

A second area that has been given inadequate attention is the entire process of decision making: How do terrorists decide what to do? What are the rules? How do they measure success and failure? What arguments are made within a terrorist group for or against any particular move? The answers to these questions become critical to the prediction of future terrorist activity. Indirect techniques will be useful for analysis of a subject in which hard data are almost never accessible.

Some of the problems that have imposed obstacles to or inhibited research into terrorism stem from the lack of a precise, widely accepted definition of terrorism. Consistent definitions are necessary to interdisciplinary study and crossnational utility of data. How one defines terrorism reveals what he believes the terrorist is. Some even feel that terrorism is not a topic but an artificial invention. Is there anything beyond similiarity of tactics that one might study between members of the Baader-Meinhoff gang, the Red Brigades, and other groups?

Some observers believe that terrorism may be an ephemeral problem, one that is fashionable now but that is likely to go away. Some believe that the study of terrorism is somehow unsavory, that research in this area smacks of headline-chasing or is likely to lead to social repression through the development of the equivalent of a *1984* mentality.

The fact is that the study of terrorism requires a multidisciplinary approach. Yet most of the work currently being done is by individuals. It is very difficult to find an individual who possesses all of the prerequisite skills and is willing to go far out on a scientific limb to advance his theories.

The waxing and waning of government interest also have been a problem. The larger research efforts depend on government or corporate funding, but governments are notoriously unreliable and corporations primarily are interested in the problem of physical security.

SUMMARY

To summarize, research has been sparse in data, with arguments supported for the most part by anecdotes rather than empirical evidence. There is no central body of accepted truth, no set of axioms, no Freud, Einstein, or Darwin. Although a body of theoretical literature is gradually emerging, we are still light in methodology. Much of the research taking place is either overtly or covertly ideological. Conspiracy theories abound, whether they relate terrorism to some central direction or to the fine hand of Moscow behind every event. Such theories can be very popular.

Some useful exchange is beginning to take place, particularly over the past two or three years. The most useful and productive work has been related to the handling of hostage situations and in the area of victimology. The greatest lack of basic research has to do with terrorist behavior and decision making. Psychiatrists, other mental health professionals, and related students of human behavior could make a major contribution to this area.

Appendix A

Ethical Dimensions of Psychiatric
Intervention in Terrorist and
Hostage Situations

Appendix A

Ethical Dimensions of Psychiatric Intervention in Terrorist and Hostage Situations: A Report of the APA Task Force on Terrorism and Its Victims

The American Psychiatric Association's Task Force on Terrorism and Its Victims has examined the ethical implications of psychiatric intervention in terrorist and hostage-taking situations. The process has had several facets. First, the Task Force has collected examples of ethical conflicts that might be encountered or have already been encountered by psychiatrists in hostage situations. Second, Task Force members have discussed their personal perception of ethical conflict areas and attempts to resolve them. Third, the Task Force has been aided by the participation of involved individuals with professional experience in terrorist or hostage situations at the symposium sponsored by the American Psychiatric Association and the Law Enforcement Assistance Administration that was held in September 1979 in Baltimore, Maryland. Our collection of data from involved professionals has continued at subsequent meetings of the Task Force. We have also been assisted through parallel efforts of other professional groups, notably the report of the American Psychological Association's Task Force on the Role of Psychology in the Criminal Justice System.[1]

In terrorist and hostage situations the psychiatrist may find himself or herself acting under the extreme pressure of time and events, isolated from traditional sources of peer consultation and review by security restrictions, and operating in an area where opinions are strongly held and relevant precedents are few. Even after careful analysis supplemented by peer review, a psychiatrist may find that a given issue cannot be readily resolved. The ethical dilemma may not be a simple conflict between right and wrong but, instead, a complex balancing of valid rights of different parties and sometimes the necessity to choose the lesser evil. In offering the following principles as an informational resource document, the Task Force seeks to share with colleagues the perspectives that we have found most useful.

In those circumstances where the psychiatrist is functioning in the role of a clinician, most specifically where he or she engages in a direct physician-patient relationship, the Task Force acknowledges that all elements of the American Medical Association's Principles of Medical Ethics with Annotations Especially Applicable to Psychiatry[2] *should be upheld.*

Although the *Principles* do not specifically mention terrorist or hostage situations, they do contain relevant ethical guidelines. Section I states that "a physician shall be dedicated to providing competent medical service with compassion and respect for human dignity." In a terrorist or hostage situation compassion and respect are required not only for the victims or hostages but for the terrorist or hostage-taker and also for the law enforcement or military personnel who are attempting to resolve the situation. This broadened definition of physician responsibility is explicitly acknowledged in the *Principles:* "A physician must recognize responsibility not only to patients, but also to society, to other health professionals, and to self."

The psychiatrist may be helped in making decisions about competing needs for professional compassion and respect in a terrorist or hostage situation through attempts to maintain fidelity to his or her healing role. This role is clearest when a victim solicits treatment after a hostage-taking or terrorist incident, when the goal is to minimize the trauma and facilitate return to normal social functioning. The physician role also applies if a patient currently in therapy with a psychiatrist becomes involved in an incident as hostage or hostage-taker. In such situations, the involvement of the psychiatrist may be direct or indirect in accordance with his or her clinical judgment of the competing needs of the situation. This may include sharing clinical information, as stated in the *Principles:* "Psychiatrists at times may find it necessary, in order to protect the patient or the community from imminent danger, to reveal confidential information disclosed by the patient."

When a psychiatrist intervenes outside of a patient-physician relationship or is called on to offer professional expertise outside the practice of psychiatry as a healing art and science, he or she must be guided by broader ethical principles. This includes situations where psychiatrists act as employees of or consultants to government agencies. The *Principles* explicitly approve of psychiatric consultation to government but also emphasize the importance of clarifying one's specific role in each situation. Is the psychiatrist speaking as a dedicated citizen, individual clinician, or spokesperson for or employee of an official group?

Psychiatrists who are employees of or consultants to government agencies or private organizations should be free to decline specific interventions in terrorist or hostage incidents if in their judgment these interventions are clinically or ethically contra-indicated. If a patient with whom a psychiatrist has had an ongoing therapeutic relationship becomes involved in a terrorist or hostage incident, the psychiatrist must balance clinical and ethical reservations concerning his or her participation against the emergency nature of the situation and the possibilities for providing unique and potentially life-saving input.

Where psychiatrists are free to choose or to shape the nature of their role, there may be possibilities for forms of intervention that are positive in both the clinical and ethical sense and that validly use the psychiatrist's professional expertise in the understanding of human experience and behavior. For instance, when a psychiatrist participates in the training of law enforcement or military officers in peaceful methods of conflict resolution or in preparing responses to terrorist or hostage incidents, he or she may be genuinely serving all parties concerned, including the hostages or victims, the terrorists, law enforcement, military, or diplomatic personnel, and society at large. When the clinician is not free to choose his or her role, there are particular dangers of adopting unethical practices because of the stress of emergency situations, pressures from government officials, or attempts to serve valued ends. Psychiatrists in such situations are urged to recall that clinical ends cannot be separated from the means used to pursue them and that techniques such as intentional deception are never free from hazardous consequences for the clinicians who use them.

As in other emergency situations, the need to preserve the confidentiality of the psychiatrist-patient relationship is not an absolute one in terrorist or hostage incidents. Psychiatrists can generally make appropriate decisions in this area based on the same considerations for which confidentiality may be breached in the traditional clinical setting. The Task Force has found, however, that psychiatrists are particularly liable to error and to misinterpretation when they are given the opportunity to make statements concerning terrorist or hostage incidents to the press or broadcast media. All psychiatrists involved in this area should give careful attention to acknowledging and controlling their own needs for publicity. As stated in the *Principles:* "It is unethical for a psychiatrist to offer a professional opinion unless he/she has conducted an examination and has been granted proper authorization for such a statement."

When a psychiatrist serves as a consultant to an organization where his or her role is specifically defined in advance as partly or wholly nonclinical, the psychiatrist must be cognizant of the difficulties in divesting himself or herself of the social expectations and technical knowledge inherent in the physician role. The realistic importance, widespread publicity, and high emotional pitch of terrorist and hostage incidents may make it difficult for the psychiatrist-consultant to maintain sound personal and professional humility. Even where the psychiatrist realizes his or her limitations, however, the professional isolation inherent in these situations imposes a heavy burden on the individual clinician. The Task Force encourages individual psychiatrists to seek peer counsel in assessing the ethical and professional complexities and limits of intervention techniques. Realistic concerns about security issues should not prohibit the clinician from obtaining such counsel because these are the situations in which it may be most needed and because other clinicians with appropriate security clearances do exist. Finally, the Task Force will continue to offer ongoing consultation to psychiatrists and other clinicians who request it.

REFERENCES

1. Report of the Task Force on the Role of Psychology in the Criminal Justice System. *Am. Psychol* 33:1099–1113, 1978.
2. *The Principles of Medical Ethics with Annotations Especially Applicable to Psychiatry.* Washington, DC: American Psychiatric Association, 1981.